WALKING WITH A PURPOSE

A New Beginning belongs to..

Name

Phone

Email

Address

D Iamond Bright
ASSISTANT

begin,
blossom,
become.

2024
CALENDAR

JANUARY

S	M	T	W	T	F	S
	1	2	3	4	5	6
7	8	9	10	11	12	13
14	15	16	17	18	19	20
21	22	23	24	25	26	27
28	29	30	31			

FEBRUARY

S	M	T	W	T	F	S
				1	2	3
4	5	6	7	8	9	10
11	12	13	14	15	16	17
18	19	20	21	22	23	24
25	26	27	28	29		

MARCH

S	M	T	W	T	F	S
					1	2
3	4	5	6	7	8	9
10	11	12	13	14	15	16
17	18	19	20	21	22	23
24	25	26	27	28	29	30
31						

APRIL

S	M	T	W	T	F	S
	1	2	3	4	5	6
7	8	9	10	11	12	13
14	15	16	17	18	19	20
21	22	23	24	25	26	27
28	29	30				

MAY

S	M	T	W	T	F	S
			1	2	3	4
5	6	7	8	9	10	11
12	13	14	15	16	17	18
19	20	21	22	23	24	25
26	27	28	29	30	31	

JUNE

S	M	T	W	T	F	S
						1
2	3	4	5	6	7	8
9	10	11	12	13	14	15
16	17	18	19	20	21	22
23	24	25	26	27	28	29
30						

JULY

S	M	T	W	T	F	S
	1	2	3	4	5	6
7	8	9	10	11	12	13
14	15	16	17	18	19	20
21	22	23	24	25	26	27
28	29	30	31			

AUGUST

S	M	T	W	T	F	S
				1	2	3
4	5	6	7	8	9	10
11	12	13	14	15	16	17
18	19	20	21	22	23	24
25	26	27	28	29	30	31

SEPTEMBER

S	M	T	W	T	F	S
1	2	3	4	5	6	7
8	9	10	11	12	13	14
15	16	17	18	19	20	21
22	23	24	25	26	27	28
29	30					

OCTOBER

S	M	T	W	T	F	S
		1	2	3	4	5
6	7	8	9	10	11	12
13	14	15	16	17	18	19
20	21	22	23	24	25	26
27	28	29	30	31		

NOVEMBER

S	M	T	W	T	F	S
					1	2
3	4	5	6	7	8	9
10	11	12	13	14	15	16
17	18	19	20	21	22	23
24	25	26	27	28	29	30

DECEMBER

S	M	T	W	T	F	S
1	2	3	4	5	6	7
8	9	10	11	12	13	14
15	16	17	18	19	20	21
22	23	24	25	26	27	28
29	30	31				

2025

CALENDAR

JANUARY

S	M	T	W	T	F	S
			1	2	3	4
5	6	7	8	9	10	11
12	13	14	15	16	17	18
19	20	21	22	23	24	25
26	27	28	29	30	31	

FEBRUARY

S	M	T	W	T	F	S
						1
2	3	4	5	6	7	8
9	10	11	12	13	14	15
16	17	18	19	20	21	22
23	24	25	26	27	28	

MARCH

S	M	T	W	T	F	S
						1
2	3	4	5	6	7	8
9	10	11	12	13	14	15
16	17	18	19	20	21	22
23	24	25	26	27	28	29
30	31					

APRIL

S	M	T	W	T	F	S
		1	2	3	4	5
6	7	8	9	10	11	12
13	14	15	16	17	18	19
20	21	22	23	24	25	26
27	28	29	30			

MAY

S	M	T	W	T	F	S
				1	2	3
4	5	6	7	8	9	10
11	12	13	14	15	16	17
18	19	20	21	22	23	24
25	26	27	28	29	30	31

JUNE

S	M	T	W	T	F	S
1	2	3	4	5	6	7
8	9	10	11	12	13	14
15	16	17	18	19	20	21
22	23	24	25	26	27	28
29	30					

JULY

S	M	T	W	T	F	S
		1	2	3	4	5
6	7	8	9	10	11	12
13	14	15	16	17	18	19
20	21	22	23	24	25	26
27	28	29	30	31		

AUGUST

S	M	T	W	T	F	S
					1	2
3	4	5	6	7	8	9
10	11	12	13	14	15	16
17	18	19	20	21	22	23
24	25	26	27	28	29	30
31						

SEPTEMBER

S	M	T	W	T	F	S
	1	2	3	4	5	6
7	8	9	10	11	12	13
14	15	16	17	18	19	20
21	22	23	24	25	26	27
28	29	30				

OCTOBER

S	M	T	W	T	F	S
			1	2	3	4
5	6	7	8	9	10	11
12	13	14	15	16	17	18
19	20	21	22	23	24	25
26	27	28	29	30	31	

NOVEMBER

S	M	T	W	T	F	S
						1
2	3	4	5	6	7	8
9	10	11	12	13	14	15
16	17	18	19	20	21	22
23	24	25	26	27	28	29
30						

DECEMBER

S	M	T	W	T	F	S
	1	2	3	4	5	6
7	8	9	10	11	12	13
14	15	16	17	18	19	20
21	22	23	24	25	26	27
28	29	30	31			

2026 CALENDAR

JANUARY

S	M	T	W	T	F	S
				1	2	3
4	5	6	7	8	9	10
11	12	13	14	15	16	17
18	19	20	21	22	23	24
25	26	27	28	29	30	31

FEBRUARY

S	M	T	W	T	F	S
1	2	3	4	5	6	7
8	9	10	11	12	13	14
15	16	17	18	19	20	21
22	23	24	25	26	27	28

MARCH

S	M	T	W	T	F	S
1	2	3	4	5	6	7
8	9	10	11	12	13	14
15	16	17	18	19	20	21
22	23	24	25	26	27	28
29	30	31				

APRIL

S	M	T	W	T	F	S
			1	2	3	4
5	6	7	8	9	10	11
12	13	14	15	16	17	18
19	20	21	22	23	24	25
26	27	28	29	30		

MAY

S	M	T	W	T	F	S
					1	2
3	4	5	6	7	8	9
10	11	12	13	14	15	16
17	18	19	20	21	22	23
24	25	26	27	28	29	30
31						

JUNE

S	M	T	W	T	F	S
	1	2	3	4	5	6
7	8	9	10	11	12	13
14	15	16	17	18	19	20
21	22	23	24	25	26	27
28	29	30				

JULY

S	M	T	W	T	F	S
			1	2	3	4
5	6	7	8	9	10	11
12	13	14	15	16	17	18
19	20	21	22	23	24	25
26	27	28	29	30	31	

AUGUST

S	M	T	W	T	F	S
						1
2	3	4	5	6	7	8
9	10	11	12	13	14	15
16	17	18	19	20	21	22
23	24	25	26	27	28	29
30	31					

SEPTEMBER

S	M	T	W	T	F	S
		1	2	3	4	5
6	7	8	9	10	11	12
13	14	15	16	17	18	19
20	21	22	23	24	25	26
27	28	29	30			

OCTOBER

S	M	T	W	T	F	S
				1	2	3
4	5	6	7	8	9	10
11	12	13	14	15	16	17
18	19	20	21	22	23	24
25	26	27	28	29	30	31

NOVEMBER

S	M	T	W	T	F	S
1	2	3	4	5	6	7
8	9	10	11	12	13	14
15	16	17	18	19	20	21
22	23	24	25	26	27	28
29	30					

DECEMBER

S	M	T	W	T	F	S
		1	2	3	4	5
6	7	8	9	10	11	12
13	14	15	16	17	18	19
20	21	22	23	24	25	26
27	28	29	30	31		

YEARLY PLANNER

JANUARY	FEBRUARY	MARCH

APRIL	MAY	JUNE

JULY	AUGUST	SEPTEMBER

OCTOBER	NOVEMBER	DECEMBER

YEARLY VISION

WHAT I WANT MY LIFE TO LOOK LIKE IN A YEAR:

ACTIONS I NEED TO TAKE TO ACHIEVE MY VISION:

MY MOTIVATION FOR ACHIEVING MY VISION:

GOAL TRACKER

Goal

Motivation

Start Date: Projected Due Date: Duration:

Action Plan

Date **Action Steps**

Roadblocks

Progress Bar: Date Completed:

Goal

Motivation

Start Date: Projected Due Date: Duration:

Action Plan

Date **Action Steps**

Roadblocks

Progress Bar: Date Completed:

GOAL TRACKER

Goal

Motivation

Start Date: Projected Due Date: Duration:

Action Plan

Date **Action Steps**

Roadblocks

Progress Bar: Date Completed:

Goal

Motivation

Start Date: Projected Due Date: Duration:

Action Plan

Date **Action Steps**

Roadblocks

Progress Bar: Date Completed:

GOAL TRACKER

Goal

Motivation

Start Date: Projected Due Date: Duration:

Action Plan

Date **Action Steps**

Roadblocks

Progress Bar: ○ ○ ○ ○ ○ ○ ○ ○ ○ ○ Date Completed:

Goal

Motivation

Start Date: Projected Due Date: Duration:

Action Plan

Date **Action Steps**

Roadblocks

Progress Bar: ○ ○ ○ ○ ○ ○ ○ ○ ○ ○ Date Completed:

GOAL TRACKER

Goal

Motivation

Start Date: Projected Due Date: Duration:

Action Plan

Date **Action Steps**

Roadblocks

Progress Bar: Date Completed:

Goal

Motivation

Start Date: Projected Due Date: Duration:

Action Plan

Date **Action Steps**

Roadblocks

Progress Bar: Date Completed:

PROJECT PLANNER

PROJECT NAME

CLIENT NAME	START DATE	DUE DATE

PROJECT OVERVIEW

PROJECT GOALS

-
-
-

-
-
-

PROJECT STRATEGY

-
-
-

RESOURCE & IDEAS

-
-
-

WORK PROGRESS	10%	20%	30%	40%	50%	60%	70%	80%	90%	100%

IMPORTANT NOTES

PROJECT PLANNER

PROJECT NAME

CLIENT NAME	START DATE	DUE DATE

PROJECT OVERVIEW

PROJECT GOALS

-
-
-

-
-
-

PROJECT STRATEGY

-
-
-

RESOURCE & IDEAS

-
-
-

WORK PROGRESS	10%	20%	30%	40%	50%	60%	70%	80%	90%	100%

IMPORTANT NOTES

PROJECT PLANNER

PROJECT NAME

CLIENT NAME	START DATE	DUE DATE

PROJECT OVERVIEW

PROJECT GOALS

-
-
-
-
-
-

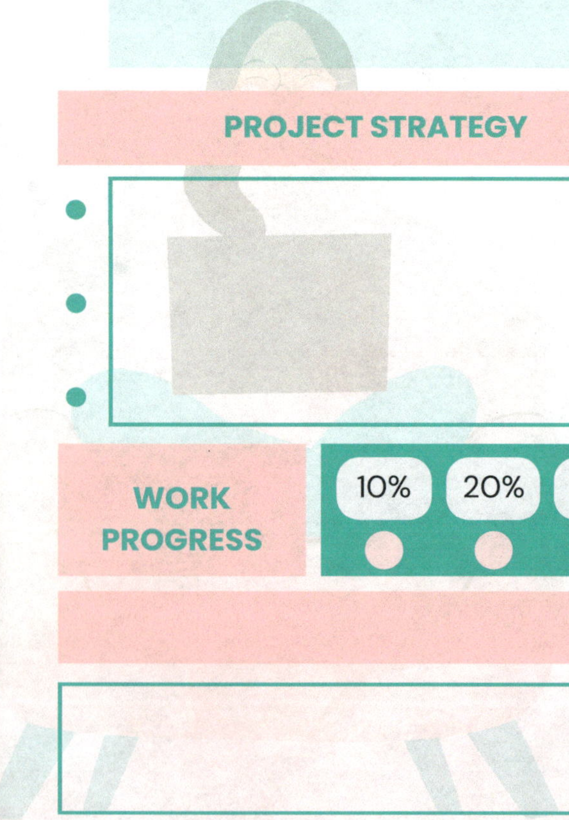

PROJECT STRATEGY

-
-
-

RESOURCE & IDEAS

-
-
-

WORK PROGRESS	10%	20%	30%	40%	50%	60%	70%	80%	90%	100%

IMPORTANT NOTES

PROJECT PLANNER

PROJECT NAME

CLIENT NAME	START DATE	DUE DATE

PROJECT OVERVIEW

PROJECT GOALS

-
-
-

-
-
-

PROJECT STRATEGY

-
-
-

RESOURCE & IDEAS

-
-
-

WORK PROGRESS	10%	20%	30%	40%	50%	60%	70%	80%	90%	100%

IMPORTANT NOTES

JANUARY

Monday	Tuesday	Wednesday	Thursday

To-Do

-
-
-
-
-
-
-
-
-
-
-
-
-
-

Affirmations For The month

Important Dates

Habits

To start	To stop

What do I love about myself?

Friday	Saturday	Sunday

Self-Care Activities

Main Goals

Appointments

Notes

JANUARY BUDGET

Source Of Income	Amount
	$
	$
	$
Total Income	$

Expenses

Date	Bills	Budget	Actual
		$	$
		$	$
		$	$
		$	$
		$	$
		$	$
		$	$
		$	$
		$	$
		$	$
Total		$	$

Date	Groceries	Budget	Actual
		$	$
		$	$
		$	$
		$	$
		$	$
		$	$
		$	$
Total		$	$

Date	Transportation	Budget	Actual
		$	$
		$	$
		$	$
Total		$	$

Date	Shopping	Budget	Actual
		$	$
		$	$
		$	$
		$	$
		$	$
		$	$
Total		$	$

Date	Entertainment	Budget	Actual
		$	$
		$	$
		$	$
Total		$	$

Date	Fees & Charges	Budget	Actual
		$	$
		$	$
		$	$
Total		$	$

Date	Saving	Goal	Needed
		$	$
		$	$
		$	$
Total		$	$

TIME TRACKER

Use a green marker to highlight the hours you are focused and working on your goals. Over the course of the month – revisit and see what your productivity looks like.

DATE	AM												PM											
1	1	2	3	4	5	6	7	8	9	10	11	12	1	2	3	4	5	6	7	8	9	10	11	12
2	1	2	3	4	5	6	7	8	9	10	11	12	1	2	3	4	5	6	7	8	9	10	11	12
3	1	2	3	4	5	6	7	8	9	10	11	12	1	2	3	4	5	6	7	8	9	10	11	12
4	1	2	3	4	5	6	7	8	9	10	11	12	1	2	3	4	5	6	7	8	9	10	11	12
5	1	2	3	4	5	6	7	8	9	10	11	12	1	2	3	4	5	6	7	8	9	10	11	12
6	1	2	3	4	5	6	7	8	9	10	11	12	1	2	3	4	5	6	7	8	9	10	11	12
7	1	2	3	4	5	6	7	8	9	10	11	12	1	2	3	4	5	6	7	8	9	10	11	12
8	1	2	3	4	5	6	7	8	9	10	11	12	1	2	3	4	5	6	7	8	9	10	11	12
9	1	2	3	4	5	6	7	8	9	10	11	12	1	2	3	4	5	6	7	8	9	10	11	12
10	1	2	3	4	5	6	7	8	9	10	11	12	1	2	3	4	5	6	7	8	9	10	11	12
11	1	2	3	4	5	6	7	8	9	10	11	12	1	2	3	4	5	6	7	8	9	10	11	12
12	1	2	3	4	5	6	7	8	9	10	11	12	1	2	3	4	5	6	7	8	9	10	11	12
13	1	2	3	4	5	6	7	8	9	10	11	12	1	2	3	4	5	6	7	8	9	10	11	12
14	1	2	3	4	5	6	7	8	9	10	11	12	1	2	3	4	5	6	7	8	9	10	11	12
15	1	2	3	4	5	6	7	8	9	10	11	12	1	2	3	4	5	6	7	8	9	10	11	12
16	1	2	3	4	5	6	7	8	9	10	11	12	1	2	3	4	5	6	7	8	9	10	11	12
17	1	2	3	4	5	6	7	8	9	10	11	12	1	2	3	4	5	6	7	8	9	10	11	12
18	1	2	3	4	5	6	7	8	9	10	11	12	1	2	3	4	5	6	7	8	9	10	11	12
19	1	2	3	4	5	6	7	8	9	10	11	12	1	2	3	4	5	6	7	8	9	10	11	12
20	1	2	3	4	5	6	7	8	9	10	11	12	1	2	3	4	5	6	7	8	9	10	11	12
21	1	2	3	4	5	6	7	8	9	10	11	12	1	2	3	4	5	6	7	8	9	10	11	12
22	1	2	3	4	5	6	7	8	9	10	11	12	1	2	3	4	5	6	7	8	9	10	11	12
23	1	2	3	4	5	6	7	8	9	10	11	12	1	2	3	4	5	6	7	8	9	10	11	12
24	1	2	3	4	5	6	7	8	9	10	11	12	1	2	3	4	5	6	7	8	9	10	11	12
25	1	2	3	4	5	6	7	8	9	10	11	12	1	2	3	4	5	6	7	8	9	10	11	12
26	1	2	3	4	5	6	7	8	9	10	11	12	1	2	3	4	5	6	7	8	9	10	11	12
27	1	2	3	4	5	6	7	8	9	10	11	12	1	2	3	4	5	6	7	8	9	10	11	12
28	1	2	3	4	5	6	7	8	9	10	11	12	1	2	3	4	5	6	7	8	9	10	11	12
29	1	2	3	4	5	6	7	8	9	10	11	12	1	2	3	4	5	6	7	8	9	10	11	12
30	1	2	3	4	5	6	7	8	9	10	11	12	1	2	3	4	5	6	7	8	9	10	11	12
31	1	2	3	4	5	6	7	8	9	10	11	12	1	2	3	4	5	6	7	8	9	10	11	12

CLIENT INFORMATION

Name
Phone
Email
Website
Address
Billing Adress
City
State Zip
D.O.B
Business Hours

Additional Information

Name
Phone
Email
Website
Address
Billing Adress
City
State Zip
D.O.B
Business Hours

Additional Information

Name
Phone
Email
Website
Address
Billing Adress
City
State Zip
D.O.B
Business Hours

Additional Information

Name
Phone
Email
Website
Address
Billing Adress
City
State Zip
D.O.B
Business Hours

Additional Information

CLIENT INFORMATION

Name
Phone
Email
Website
Address
Billing Adress
City
State Zip
D.O.B
Business Hours

Additional Information

Name
Phone
Email
Website
Address
Billing Adress
City
State Zip
D.O.B
Business Hours

Additional Information

Name
Phone
Email
Website
Address
Billing Adress
City
State Zip
D.O.B
Business Hours

Additional Information

Name
Phone
Email
Website
Address
Billing Adress
City
State Zip
D.O.B
Business Hours

Additional Information

MEETING NOTES

SUBJECT	DATE	TIME

AGENDA

ATTENDEES

-
-
-
-
-

IMPORTANT NOTES

SUBJECT	DATE	TIME

AGENDA

ATTENDEES

-
-
-
-
-

IMPORTANT NOTES

MEETING NOTES

SUBJECT	DATE	TIME

AGENDA

ATTENDEES

-
-
-
-
-

IMPORTANT NOTES

SUBJECT	DATE	TIME

AGENDA

ATTENDEES

-
-
-
-
-

IMPORTANT NOTES

JANUARY SELF-CARE

Write a self-care activity and tick off each time you do self-care act.

ACTIVITIES	CHECKLIST
	1 2 3 4 5 6 7 8 9 10 11 12 13 14 15 16 17 18 19 20 21 22 23 24 25 26 27 28 29 30 31
	1 2 3 4 5 6 7 8 9 10 11 12 13 14 15 16 17 18 19 20 21 22 23 24 25 26 27 28 29 30 31
	1 2 3 4 5 6 7 8 9 10 11 12 13 14 15 16 17 18 19 20 21 22 23 24 25 26 27 28 29 30 31
	1 2 3 4 5 6 7 8 9 10 11 12 13 14 15 16 17 18 19 20 21 22 23 24 25 26 27 28 29 30 31
	1 2 3 4 5 6 7 8 9 10 11 12 13 14 15 16 17 18 19 20 21 22 23 24 25 26 27 28 29 30 31
	1 2 3 4 5 6 7 8 9 10 11 12 13 14 15 16 17 18 19 20 21 22 23 24 25 26 27 28 29 30 31
	1 2 3 4 5 6 7 8 9 10 11 12 13 14 15 16 17 18 19 20 21 22 23 24 25 26 27 28 29 30 31
	1 2 3 4 5 6 7 8 9 10 11 12 13 14 15 16 17 18 19 20 21 22 23 24 25 26 27 28 29 30 31
	1 2 3 4 5 6 7 8 9 10 11 12 13 14 15 16 17 18 19 20 21 22 23 24 25 26 27 28 29 30 31
	1 2 3 4 5 6 7 8 9 10 11 12 13 14 15 16 17 18 19 20 21 22 23 24 25 26 27 28 29 30 31

REFLECTION

HOW WILL YOU RATE THIS MONTH? ☆ ☆ ☆ ☆ ☆ ☆ ☆ ☆ ☆ ☆

MONTHLY WINS	HOW DOES IT MAKE ME FEEL?
•	•
•	•
•	•
•	•

CHALLENGES	HOW CAN I IMPROVE IT?
•	•
•	•
•	•
•	•

ACCOMPLISHED GOALS	UNACCOMPLISHED GOALS	GOALS NEXT MONTH

HABITS RETAINED	HABITS ELIMINATED	NEW HABITS DEVELOPED

THREE THINGS THAT I AM MOST GRATEFUL FOR THIS MONTH

1	2	3

TWO LIFE LESSONS I LEARNED THIS MONTH

1	2

ONE WORD THAT BEST DESCRIBES THIS MONTH

WEEKLY PLANNER

WEEK OF

MOTIVATION

MON

TUE

WED

THUR

FRI

SAT

SUN

TO-DO

TOP PRIORITIES

NOTES

DAILY PLANNER

DATE S M T W T F S

TODAY'S GOALS

TODAY APPOINTMENT

Time	Event

SLEEP

MOOD

WATER INTAKE

Total :

EXERCISE

Total Minutes

Total Steps

MEAL TRACKER

Breakfast

Lunch

Dinner

Snack

THINGS TO GET DONE TODAY

REMINDER

MONEY TRACKER

Money In

Money Out

TODAY I'M GRATEFUL FOR

NOTES

DAILY PLANNER

DATE

S M T W T F S

TODAY'S GOALS

TODAY APPOINTMENT

Time	Event

SLEEP

MOOD

WATER INTAKE

Total :

EXERCISE

Total Minutes

Total Steps

MEAL TRACKER

Breakfast

Lunch

Dinner

Snack

THINGS TO GET DONE TODAY

REMINDER

MONEY TRACKER

Money In	Money Out

TODAY I'M GRATEFUL FOR

NOTES

DAILY PLANNER

DATE S M T W T F S

TODAY'S GOALS

TODAY APPOINTMENT

Time	Event

SLEEP

MOOD

WATER INTAKE

Total :

EXERCISE

Total Minutes

Total Steps

MEAL TRACKER

Breakfast

Lunch

Dinner

Snack

THINGS TO GET DONE TODAY

REMINDER

MONEY TRACKER

Money In

Money Out

TODAY I'M GRATEFUL FOR

NOTES

DAILY PLANNER

DATE

S M T W T F S

TODAY'S GOALS

TODAY APPOINTMENT

Time	Event

SLEEP

MOOD

WATER INTAKE

Total :

EXERCISE

Total Minutes

Total Steps

THINGS TO GET DONE TODAY

MEAL TRACKER

Breakfast

Lunch

Dinner

Snack

REMINDER

MONEY TRACKER

Money In	Money Out

TODAY I'M GRATEFUL FOR

NOTES

DAILY PLANNER

DATE S M T W T F S

TODAY'S GOALS

TODAY APPOINTMENT

Time	Event

SLEEP

MOOD

WATER INTAKE

Total :

EXERCISE

Total Minutes

Total Steps

MEAL TRACKER

Breakfast

Lunch

Dinner

Snack

THINGS TO GET DONE TODAY

REMINDER

TODAY I'M GRATEFUL FOR

NOTES

MONEY TRACKER

Money In	Money Out

DAILY PLANNER

DATE

S M T W T F S

TODAY'S GOALS

TODAY APPOINTMENT

Time	Event

SLEEP

MOOD

WATER INTAKE

Total :

EXERCISE

Total Minutes

Total Steps

THINGS TO GET DONE TODAY

MEAL TRACKER

Breakfast

Lunch

Dinner

Snack

REMINDER

TODAY I'M GRATEFUL FOR

NOTES

MONEY TRACKER

Money In	Money Out

DAILY PLANNER

DATE S M T W T F S

TODAY'S GOALS

TODAY APPOINTMENT

Time	Event

SLEEP

MOOD

WATER INTAKE

Total :

EXERCISE

Total Minutes

Total Steps

MEAL TRACKER

Breakfast

Lunch

Dinner

Snack

THINGS TO GET DONE TODAY

REMINDER

MONEY TRACKER

Money In

Money Out

TODAY I'M GRATEFUL FOR

NOTES

WEEKLY PLANNER

WEEK OF

MOTIVATION

MON

TUE

WED

THUR

FRI

SAT

SUN

TO-DO

TOP PRIORITIES

NOTES

DAILY PLANNER

DATE S M T W T F S

TODAY'S GOALS

TODAY APPOINTMENT

Time	Event

SLEEP

MOOD

WATER INTAKE

Total :

EXERCISE

Total Minutes

Total Steps

MEAL TRACKER

Breakfast

Lunch

Dinner

Snack

THINGS TO GET DONE TODAY

REMINDER

MONEY TRACKER

Money In	Money Out

TODAY I'M GRATEFUL FOR

NOTES

DAILY PLANNER

DATE

S M T W T F S

TODAY'S GOALS

TODAY APPOINTMENT

Time	Event

SLEEP

MOOD

WATER INTAKE

Total :

EXERCISE

Total Minutes

Total Steps

THINGS TO GET DONE TODAY

MEAL TRACKER

Breakfast

Lunch

Dinner

Snack

REMINDER

TODAY I'M GRATEFUL FOR

NOTES

MONEY TRACKER

Money In	Money Out

DAILY PLANNER

DATE S M T W T F S

TODAY'S GOALS

TODAY APPOINTMENT

Time	Event

SLEEP

MOOD

WATER INTAKE

Total :

EXERCISE

Total Minutes

Total Steps

THINGS TO GET DONE TODAY

MEAL TRACKER

Breakfast

Lunch

Dinner

Snack

REMINDER

MONEY TRACKER

Money In	Money Out

TODAY I'M GRATEFUL FOR

NOTES

DAILY PLANNER

DATE

S M T W T F S

TODAY'S GOALS

TODAY APPOINTMENT

Time	Event

SLEEP

MOOD

WATER INTAKE

Total :

EXERCISE

Total Minutes

Total Steps

THINGS TO GET DONE TODAY

MEAL TRACKER

Breakfast

Lunch

Dinner

Snack

REMINDER

TODAY I'M GRATEFUL FOR

MONEY TRACKER

Money In	Money Out

NOTES

DAILY PLANNER

DATE

S M T W T F S

TODAY'S GOALS

TODAY APPOINTMENT

Time	Event

SLEEP

MOOD

WATER INTAKE

Total :

EXERCISE

Total Minutes

Total Steps

THINGS TO GET DONE TODAY

MEAL TRACKER

Breakfast

Lunch

Dinner

Snack

REMINDER

TODAY I'M GRATEFUL FOR

NOTES

MONEY TRACKER

Money In	Money Out

DAILY PLANNER

DATE

S M T W T F S

TODAY'S GOALS

TODAY APPOINTMENT

Time	Event

SLEEP

MOOD

WATER INTAKE

Total :

THINGS TO GET DONE TODAY

EXERCISE

Total Minutes

Total Steps

MEAL TRACKER

Breakfast

Lunch

Dinner

Snack

REMINDER

TODAY I'M GRATEFUL FOR

NOTES

MONEY TRACKER

Money In	Money Out

DAILY PLANNER

DATE S M T W T F S

TODAY'S GOALS

TODAY APPOINTMENT

Time	Event

SLEEP

MOOD

WATER INTAKE

Total :

EXERCISE

Total Minutes

Total Steps

THINGS TO GET DONE TODAY

MEAL TRACKER

Breakfast

Lunch

Dinner

Snack

REMINDER

TODAY I'M GRATEFUL FOR

NOTES

MONEY TRACKER

Money In	Money Out

WEEKLY PLANNER

WEEK OF

MOTIVATION

MON

TUE

WED

THUR

FRI

SAT

SUN

TO-DO

TOP PRIORITIES

NOTES

DAILY PLANNER

DATE S M T W T F S

TODAY'S GOALS

TODAY APPOINTMENT

Time	Event

SLEEP

MOOD

WATER INTAKE

Total :

EXERCISE

Total Minutes

Total Steps

THINGS TO GET DONE TODAY

MEAL TRACKER

Breakfast

Lunch

Dinner

Snack

REMINDER

MONEY TRACKER

Money In

Money Out

TODAY I'M GRATEFUL FOR

NOTES

DAILY PLANNER

DATE

S M T W T F S

TODAY'S GOALS

TODAY APPOINTMENT

Time	Event

SLEEP

MOOD

WATER INTAKE

Total :

EXERCISE

Total Minutes

Total Steps

MEAL TRACKER

Breakfast

Lunch

Dinner

Snack

THINGS TO GET DONE TODAY

REMINDER

MONEY TRACKER

Money In	Money Out

TODAY I'M GRATEFUL FOR

NOTES

DAILY PLANNER

DATE

S M T W T F S

TODAY'S GOALS

TODAY APPOINTMENT

Time	Event

SLEEP

MOOD

WATER INTAKE

Total :

EXERCISE

Total Minutes

Total Steps

THINGS TO GET DONE TODAY

MEAL TRACKER

Breakfast

Lunch

Dinner

Snack

REMINDER

MONEY TRACKER

Money In

Money Out

TODAY I'M GRATEFUL FOR

NOTES

DAILY PLANNER

DATE

S M T W T F S

TODAY'S GOALS

TODAY APPOINTMENT

Time	Event

SLEEP

MOOD

WATER INTAKE

Total :

EXERCISE

Total Minutes

Total Steps

THINGS TO GET DONE TODAY

MEAL TRACKER

Breakfast

Lunch

Dinner

Snack

REMINDER

TODAY I'M GRATEFUL FOR

NOTES

MONEY TRACKER

Money In	Money Out

DAILY PLANNER

DATE S M T W T F S

TODAY'S GOALS

TODAY APPOINTMENT

Time	Event

SLEEP

MOOD

WATER INTAKE

Total :

EXERCISE

Total Minutes

Total Steps

MEAL TRACKER

Breakfast

Lunch

Dinner

Snack

THINGS TO GET DONE TODAY

REMINDER

MONEY TRACKER

Money In	Money Out

TODAY I'M GRATEFUL FOR

NOTES

DAILY PLANNER

DATE

S M T W T F S

TODAY'S GOALS

TODAY APPOINTMENT

Time	Event

SLEEP

MOOD

WATER INTAKE

Total :

EXERCISE

Total Minutes

Total Steps

THINGS TO GET DONE TODAY

MEAL TRACKER

Breakfast

Lunch

Dinner

Snack

REMINDER

TODAY I'M GRATEFUL FOR

NOTES

MONEY TRACKER

Money In	Money Out

DAILY PLANNER

DATE S M T W T F S

TODAY'S GOALS

TODAY APPOINTMENT

Time	Event

SLEEP

MOOD

WATER INTAKE

Total :

EXERCISE

Total Minutes

Total Steps

MEAL TRACKER

Breakfast

Lunch

Dinner

Snack

THINGS TO GET DONE TODAY

REMINDER

MONEY TRACKER

Money In	Money Out

TODAY I'M GRATEFUL FOR

NOTES

WEEKLY PLANNER

WEEK OF	
MOTIVATION	

MON

TUE

WED

THUR

FRI

SAT

SUN

TO-DO

TOP PRIORITIES

NOTES

DAILY PLANNER

DATE S M T W T F S

TODAY'S GOALS

TODAY APPOINTMENT

Time	Event

SLEEP

MOOD

WATER INTAKE

Total :

EXERCISE

Total Minutes

Total Steps

THINGS TO GET DONE TODAY

MEAL TRACKER

Breakfast

Lunch

Dinner

Snack

REMINDER

TODAY I'M GRATEFUL FOR

NOTES

MONEY TRACKER

Money In	Money Out

DAILY PLANNER

DATE

S M T W T F S

TODAY'S GOALS

TODAY APPOINTMENT

Time	Event

SLEEP

MOOD

WATER INTAKE

Total :

THINGS TO GET DONE TODAY

EXERCISE

Total Minutes

Total Steps

MEAL TRACKER

Breakfast

Lunch

Dinner

Snack

REMINDER

TODAY I'M GRATEFUL FOR

NOTES

MONEY TRACKER

Money In	Money Out

DAILY PLANNER

DATE S M T W T F S

TODAY'S GOALS

TODAY APPOINTMENT

Time	Event

SLEEP

MOOD

WATER INTAKE

Total :

EXERCISE

Total Minutes

Total Steps

THINGS TO GET DONE TODAY

MEAL TRACKER

Breakfast

Lunch

Dinner

Snack

REMINDER

TODAY I'M GRATEFUL FOR

NOTES

MONEY TRACKER

Money In	Money Out

DAILY PLANNER

DATE

S M T W T F S

TODAY'S GOALS

TODAY APPOINTMENT

Time	Event

SLEEP

MOOD

WATER INTAKE

Total :

EXERCISE

Total Minutes

Total Steps

THINGS TO GET DONE TODAY

MEAL TRACKER

Breakfast

Lunch

Dinner

Snack

REMINDER

TODAY I'M GRATEFUL FOR

NOTES

MONEY TRACKER

Money In	Money Out

DAILY PLANNER

DATE S M T W T F S

TODAY'S GOALS

TODAY APPOINTMENT

Time	Event

SLEEP

MOOD

WATER INTAKE

Total :

EXERCISE

Total Minutes

Total Steps

THINGS TO GET DONE TODAY

MEAL TRACKER

Breakfast

Lunch

Dinner

Snack

REMINDER

TODAY I'M GRATEFUL FOR

NOTES

MONEY TRACKER

Money In	Money Out

DAILY PLANNER

DATE

S M T W T F S

TODAY'S GOALS

TODAY APPOINTMENT

Time	Event

SLEEP

MOOD

WATER INTAKE

Total :

EXERCISE

Total Minutes

Total Steps

MEAL TRACKER

Breakfast

Lunch

Dinner

Snack

THINGS TO GET DONE TODAY

REMINDER

TODAY I'M GRATEFUL FOR

NOTES

MONEY TRACKER

Money In

Money Out

DAILY PLANNER

DATE S M T W T F S

TODAY'S GOALS

TODAY APPOINTMENT

Time	Event

SLEEP

MOOD

WATER INTAKE

Total :

EXERCISE

Total Minutes

Total Steps

THINGS TO GET DONE TODAY

MEAL TRACKER

Breakfast

Lunch

Dinner

Snack

REMINDER

MONEY TRACKER

Money In	Money Out

TODAY I'M GRATEFUL FOR

NOTES

DAILY PLANNER

DATE

S M T W T F S

TODAY'S GOALS

TODAY APPOINTMENT

Time	Event

SLEEP

MOOD

WATER INTAKE

Total :

EXERCISE

Total Minutes

Total Steps

THINGS TO GET DONE TODAY

MEAL TRACKER

Breakfast

Lunch

Dinner

Snack

REMINDER

TODAY I'M GRATEFUL FOR

MONEY TRACKER

Money In

Money Out

NOTES

DAILY PLANNER

DATE S M T W T F S

TODAY'S GOALS

TODAY APPOINTMENT

Time	Event

SLEEP

MOOD

WATER INTAKE

Total :

EXERCISE

Total Minutes

Total Steps

MEAL TRACKER

Breakfast

Lunch

Dinner

Snack

THINGS TO GET DONE TODAY

REMINDER

MONEY TRACKER

Money In	Money Out

TODAY I'M GRATEFUL FOR

NOTES

DAILY PLANNER

DATE

S M T W T F S

TODAY'S GOALS

TODAY APPOINTMENT

Time	Event

SLEEP

MOOD

WATER INTAKE

Total :

EXERCISE

Total Minutes

Total Steps

THINGS TO GET DONE TODAY

MEAL TRACKER

Breakfast

Lunch

Dinner

Snack

REMINDER

TODAY I'M GRATEFUL FOR

NOTES

MONEY TRACKER

Money In	Money Out

NOTES

FEBRUARY

Monday	Tuesday	Wednesday	Thursday

To-Do

Affirmations For The month

Important Dates

Habits

To start	To stop

What do I love about myself?

Friday | Saturday | Sunday

Self-Care Activities

Main Goals

Appointments

Notes

FEBRUARY BUDGET

Source Of Income	Amount
	$
	$
	$
Total Income	$

Expenses

Date	Bills	Budget	Actual
		$	$
		$	$
		$	$
		$	$
		$	$
		$	$
		$	$
		$	$
		$	$
		$	$
Total		$	$

Date	Groceries	Budget	Actual
		$	$
		$	$
		$	$
		$	$
		$	$
		$	$
		$	$
Total		$	$

Date	Transportation	Budget	Actual
		$	$
		$	$
		$	$
Total		$	$

Date	Shopping	Budget	Actual
		$	$
		$	$
		$	$
		$	$
		$	$
		$	$
Total		$	$

Date	Entertainment	Budget	Actual
		$	$
		$	$
		$	$
Total		$	$

Date	Fees & Charges	Budget	Actual
		$	$
		$	$
		$	$
Total		$	$

Date	Saving	Goal	Needed
		$	$
		$	$
		$	$
Total		$	$

TIME TRACKER

Use a green marker to highlight the hours you are focused and working on your goals. Over the course of the month – revisit and see what your productivity looks like.

DATE	AM												PM											
1	1	2	3	4	5	6	7	8	9	10	11	12	1	2	3	4	5	6	7	8	9	10	11	12
2	1	2	3	4	5	6	7	8	9	10	11	12	1	2	3	4	5	6	7	8	9	10	11	12
3	1	2	3	4	5	6	7	8	9	10	11	12	1	2	3	4	5	6	7	8	9	10	11	12
4	1	2	3	4	5	6	7	8	9	10	11	12	1	2	3	4	5	6	7	8	9	10	11	12
5	1	2	3	4	5	6	7	8	9	10	11	12	1	2	3	4	5	6	7	8	9	10	11	12
6	1	2	3	4	5	6	7	8	9	10	11	12	1	2	3	4	5	6	7	8	9	10	11	12
7	1	2	3	4	5	6	7	8	9	10	11	12	1	2	3	4	5	6	7	8	9	10	11	12
8	1	2	3	4	5	6	7	8	9	10	11	12	1	2	3	4	5	6	7	8	9	10	11	12
9	1	2	3	4	5	6	7	8	9	10	11	12	1	2	3	4	5	6	7	8	9	10	11	12
10	1	2	3	4	5	6	7	8	9	10	11	12	1	2	3	4	5	6	7	8	9	10	11	12
11	1	2	3	4	5	6	7	8	9	10	11	12	1	2	3	4	5	6	7	8	9	10	11	12
12	1	2	3	4	5	6	7	8	9	10	11	12	1	2	3	4	5	6	7	8	9	10	11	12
13	1	2	3	4	5	6	7	8	9	10	11	12	1	2	3	4	5	6	7	8	9	10	11	12
14	1	2	3	4	5	6	7	8	9	10	11	12	1	2	3	4	5	6	7	8	9	10	11	12
15	1	2	3	4	5	6	7	8	9	10	11	12	1	2	3	4	5	6	7	8	9	10	11	12
16	1	2	3	4	5	6	7	8	9	10	11	12	1	2	3	4	5	6	7	8	9	10	11	12
17	1	2	3	4	5	6	7	8	9	10	11	12	1	2	3	4	5	6	7	8	9	10	11	12
18	1	2	3	4	5	6	7	8	9	10	11	12	1	2	3	4	5	6	7	8	9	10	11	12
19	1	2	3	4	5	6	7	8	9	10	11	12	1	2	3	4	5	6	7	8	9	10	11	12
20	1	2	3	4	5	6	7	8	9	10	11	12	1	2	3	4	5	6	7	8	9	10	11	12
21	1	2	3	4	5	6	7	8	9	10	11	12	1	2	3	4	5	6	7	8	9	10	11	12
22	1	2	3	4	5	6	7	8	9	10	11	12	1	2	3	4	5	6	7	8	9	10	11	12
23	1	2	3	4	5	6	7	8	9	10	11	12	1	2	3	4	5	6	7	8	9	10	11	12
24	1	2	3	4	5	6	7	8	9	10	11	12	1	2	3	4	5	6	7	8	9	10	11	12
25	1	2	3	4	5	6	7	8	9	10	11	12	1	2	3	4	5	6	7	8	9	10	11	12
26	1	2	3	4	5	6	7	8	9	10	11	12	1	2	3	4	5	6	7	8	9	10	11	12
27	1	2	3	4	5	6	7	8	9	10	11	12	1	2	3	4	5	6	7	8	9	10	11	12
28	1	2	3	4	5	6	7	8	9	10	11	12	1	2	3	4	5	6	7	8	9	10	11	12
29	1	2	3	4	5	6	7	8	9	10	11	12	1	2	3	4	5	6	7	8	9	10	11	12
30	1	2	3	4	5	6	7	8	9	10	11	12	1	2	3	4	5	6	7	8	9	10	11	12
31	1	2	3	4	5	6	7	8	9	10	11	12	1	2	3	4	5	6	7	8	9	10	11	12

CLIENT INFORMATION

Name
Phone
Email
Website
Address
Billing Adress
City
State Zip
D.O.B
Business Hours

Additional Information

Name
Phone
Email
Website
Address
Billing Adress
City
State Zip
D.O.B
Business Hours

Additional Information

Name
Phone
Email
Website
Address
Billing Adress
City
State Zip
D.O.B
Business Hours

Additional Information

Name
Phone
Email
Website
Address
Billing Adress
City
State Zip
D.O.B
Business Hours

Additional Information

CLIENT INFORMATION

Name
Phone
Email
Website
Address
Billing Adress
City
State Zip
D.O.B
Business Hours

Additional Information

Name
Phone
Email
Website
Address
Billing Adress
City
State Zip
D.O.B
Business Hours

Additional Information

Name
Phone
Email
Website
Address
Billing Adress
City
State Zip
D.O.B
Business Hours

Additional Information

Name
Phone
Email
Website
Address
Billing Adress
City
State Zip
D.O.B
Business Hours

Additional Information

MEETING NOTES

SUBJECT	DATE	TIME

AGENDA

ATTENDEES

IMPORTANT NOTES

SUBJECT	DATE	TIME

AGENDA

ATTENDEES

IMPORTANT NOTES

MEETING NOTES

SUBJECT	DATE	TIME

AGENDA

ATTENDEES

IMPORTANT NOTES

SUBJECT	DATE	TIME

AGENDA

ATTENDEES

IMPORTANT NOTES

FEBRUARY SELF-CARE

Write a self-care activity and tick off each time you do self-care act.

ACTIVITIES	CHECKLIST
	1 2 3 4 5 6 7 8 9 10 11 12 13 14 15 16 17 18 19 20 21 22 23 24 25 26 27 28 29 30 31
	1 2 3 4 5 6 7 8 9 10 11 12 13 14 15 16 17 18 19 20 21 22 23 24 25 26 27 28 29 30 31
	1 2 3 4 5 6 7 8 9 10 11 12 13 14 15 16 17 18 19 20 21 22 23 24 25 26 27 28 29 30 31
	1 2 3 4 5 6 7 8 9 10 11 12 13 14 15 16 17 18 19 20 21 22 23 24 25 26 27 28 29 30 31
	1 2 3 4 5 6 7 8 9 10 11 12 13 14 15 16 17 18 19 20 21 22 23 24 25 26 27 28 29 30 31
	1 2 3 4 5 6 7 8 9 10 11 12 13 14 15 16 17 18 19 20 21 22 23 24 25 26 27 28 29 30 31
	1 2 3 4 5 6 7 8 9 10 11 12 13 14 15 16 17 18 19 20 21 22 23 24 25 26 27 28 29 30 31
	1 2 3 4 5 6 7 8 9 10 11 12 13 14 15 16 17 18 19 20 21 22 23 24 25 26 27 28 29 30 31
	1 2 3 4 5 6 7 8 9 10 11 12 13 14 15 16 17 18 19 20 21 22 23 24 25 26 27 28 29 30 31
	1 2 3 4 5 6 7 8 9 10 11 12 13 14 15 16 17 18 19 20 21 22 23 24 25 26 27 28 29 30 31

REFLECTION

HOW WILL YOU RATE THIS MONTH? ☆ ☆ ☆ ☆ ☆ ☆ ☆ ☆ ☆ ☆

MONTHLY WINS

-
-
-
-

HOW DOES IT MAKE ME FEEL?

-
-
-
-

CHALLENGES

-
-
-
-

HOW CAN I IMPROVE IT?

-
-
-
-

ACCOMPLISHED GOALS	UNACCOMPLISHED GOALS	GOALS NEXT MONTH

HABITS RETAINED	HABITS ELIMINATED	NEW HABITS DEVELOPED

THREE THINGS THAT I AM MOST GRATEFUL FOR THIS MONTH

1

2

3

TWO LIFE LESSONS I LEARNED THIS MONTH

1

2

ONE WORD THAT BEST DESCRIBES THIS MONTH

WEEKLY PLANNER

WEEK OF	
MOTIVATION	

MON

TUE

WED

THUR

FRI

SAT

SUN

TO-DO

TOP PRIORITIES

NOTES

DAILY PLANNER

DATE S M T W T F S

TODAY'S GOALS

TODAY APPOINTMENT

Time	Event

SLEEP

MOOD

WATER INTAKE

Total :

EXERCISE

Total Minutes

Total Steps

MEAL TRACKER

Breakfast

Lunch

Dinner

Snack

THINGS TO GET DONE TODAY

REMINDER

TODAY I'M GRATEFUL FOR

NOTES

MONEY TRACKER

Money In	Money Out

DAILY PLANNER

DATE

S M T W T F S

TODAY'S GOALS

TODAY APPOINTMENT

Time	Event

SLEEP

MOOD

WATER INTAKE

Total :

EXERCISE

Total Minutes

Total Steps

MEAL TRACKER

Breakfast

Lunch

Dinner

Snack

THINGS TO GET DONE TODAY

REMINDER

MONEY TRACKER

Money In	Money Out

TODAY I'M GRATEFUL FOR

NOTES

DAILY PLANNER

DATE S M T W T F S

TODAY'S GOALS

TODAY APPOINTMENT

Time	Event

SLEEP

MOOD

WATER INTAKE

Total :

EXERCISE

Total Minutes

Total Steps

MEAL TRACKER

Breakfast

Lunch

Dinner

Snack

THINGS TO GET DONE TODAY

REMINDER

MONEY TRACKER

Money In	Money Out

TODAY I'M GRATEFUL FOR

NOTES

DAILY PLANNER

DATE

S M T W T F S

TODAY'S GOALS

TODAY APPOINTMENT

Time	Event

SLEEP

MOOD

WATER INTAKE

Total :

EXERCISE

Total Minutes

Total Steps

THINGS TO GET DONE TODAY

MEAL TRACKER

Breakfast

Lunch

Dinner

Snack

REMINDER

TODAY I'M GRATEFUL FOR

NOTES

MONEY TRACKER

Money In	Money Out

DAILY PLANNER

DATE S M T W T F S

TODAY'S GOALS

TODAY APPOINTMENT

Time	Event

SLEEP

MOOD

WATER INTAKE

Total :

EXERCISE

Total Minutes

Total Steps

MEAL TRACKER

Breakfast

Lunch

Dinner

Snack

THINGS TO GET DONE TODAY

REMINDER

TODAY I'M GRATEFUL FOR

NOTES

MONEY TRACKER

Money In	Money Out

DAILY PLANNER

DATE

S M T W T F S

TODAY'S GOALS

TODAY APPOINTMENT

Time	Event

SLEEP

MOOD

WATER INTAKE

Total :

EXERCISE

Total Minutes

Total Steps

THINGS TO GET DONE TODAY

MEAL TRACKER

Breakfast

Lunch

Dinner

Snack

REMINDER

TODAY I'M GRATEFUL FOR

NOTES

MONEY TRACKER

Money In	Money Out

DAILY PLANNER

DATE S M T W T F S

TODAY'S GOALS

TODAY APPOINTMENT

Time	Event

SLEEP

MOOD

WATER INTAKE

Total :

EXERCISE

Total Minutes

Total Steps

THINGS TO GET DONE TODAY

MEAL TRACKER

Breakfast

Lunch

Dinner

Snack

REMINDER

TODAY I'M GRATEFUL FOR

NOTES

MONEY TRACKER

Money In	Money Out

WEEKLY PLANNER

WEEK OF

MOTIVATION

MON

TUE

WED

THUR

FRI

SAT

SUN

TO-DO

TOP PRIORITIES

NOTES

DAILY PLANNER

DATE S M T W T F S

TODAY'S GOALS

TODAY APPOINTMENT

Time	Event

SLEEP

MOOD

WATER INTAKE

Total :

EXERCISE

Total Minutes

Total Steps

THINGS TO GET DONE TODAY

MEAL TRACKER

Breakfast

Lunch

Dinner

Snack

REMINDER

TODAY I'M GRATEFUL FOR

MONEY TRACKER

Money In	Money Out

NOTES

DAILY PLANNER

DATE

S M T W T F S

TODAY'S GOALS

TODAY APPOINTMENT

Time	Event

SLEEP

MOOD

WATER INTAKE

Total :

EXERCISE

Total Minutes

Total Steps

THINGS TO GET DONE TODAY

MEAL TRACKER

Breakfast

Lunch

Dinner

Snack

REMINDER

TODAY I'M GRATEFUL FOR

NOTES

MONEY TRACKER

Money In	Money Out

DAILY PLANNER

DATE S M T W T F S

TODAY'S GOALS

TODAY APPOINTMENT

Time	Event

SLEEP

MOOD

WATER INTAKE

Total :

EXERCISE

Total Minutes

Total Steps

THINGS TO GET DONE TODAY

MEAL TRACKER

Breakfast

Lunch

Dinner

Snack

REMINDER

TODAY I'M GRATEFUL FOR

MONEY TRACKER

Money In

Money Out

NOTES

DAILY PLANNER

DATE

S M T W T F S

TODAY'S GOALS

TODAY APPOINTMENT

Time	Event

SLEEP

MOOD

WATER INTAKE

Total :

EXERCISE

Total Minutes

Total Steps

THINGS TO GET DONE TODAY

MEAL TRACKER

Breakfast

Lunch

Dinner

Snack

REMINDER

TODAY I'M GRATEFUL FOR

NOTES

MONEY TRACKER

Money In	Money Out

DAILY PLANNER

DATE S M T W T F S

TODAY'S GOALS

TODAY APPOINTMENT

Time	Event

SLEEP

MOOD

WATER INTAKE

Total :

EXERCISE

Total Minutes

Total Steps

MEAL TRACKER

Breakfast

Lunch

Dinner

Snack

THINGS TO GET DONE TODAY

REMINDER

MONEY TRACKER

Money In

Money Out

TODAY I'M GRATEFUL FOR

NOTES

DAILY PLANNER

DATE

S M T W T F S

TODAY'S GOALS

TODAY APPOINTMENT

Time	Event

SLEEP

MOOD

WATER INTAKE

Total :

THINGS TO GET DONE TODAY

EXERCISE

Total Minutes

Total Steps

MEAL TRACKER

Breakfast

Lunch

Dinner

Snack

REMINDER

TODAY I'M GRATEFUL FOR

NOTES

MONEY TRACKER

Money In	Money Out

DAILY PLANNER

DATE S M T W T F S

TODAY'S GOALS

TODAY APPOINTMENT

Time	Event

SLEEP

MOOD

WATER INTAKE

Total :

EXERCISE

Total Minutes

Total Steps

THINGS TO GET DONE TODAY

MEAL TRACKER

Breakfast

Lunch

Dinner

Snack

REMINDER

TODAY I'M GRATEFUL FOR

NOTES

MONEY TRACKER

Money In	Money Out

WEEKLY PLANNER

WEEK OF

MOTIVATION

MON

TUE

WED

THUR

FRI

SAT

SUN

TO-DO

TOP PRIORITIES

NOTES

DAILY PLANNER

DATE S M T W T F S

TODAY'S GOALS

TODAY APPOINTMENT

Time	Event

SLEEP

MOOD

WATER INTAKE

Total :

EXERCISE

Total Minutes

Total Steps

MEAL TRACKER

Breakfast

Lunch

Dinner

Snack

THINGS TO GET DONE TODAY

REMINDER

MONEY TRACKER

Money In

Money Out

TODAY I'M GRATEFUL FOR

NOTES

DAILY PLANNER

DATE

S M T W T F S

TODAY'S GOALS

TODAY APPOINTMENT

Time	Event

SLEEP

MOOD

WATER INTAKE

Total :

EXERCISE

Total Minutes

Total Steps

THINGS TO GET DONE TODAY

MEAL TRACKER

Breakfast

Lunch

Dinner

Snack

REMINDER

TODAY I'M GRATEFUL FOR

NOTES

MONEY TRACKER

Money In	Money Out

DAILY PLANNER

DATE S M T W T F S

TODAY'S GOALS

TODAY APPOINTMENT

Time	Event

SLEEP

MOOD

WATER INTAKE

Total :

EXERCISE

Total Minutes

Total Steps

THINGS TO GET DONE TODAY

MEAL TRACKER

Breakfast

Lunch

Dinner

Snack

REMINDER

TODAY I'M GRATEFUL FOR

NOTES

MONEY TRACKER

Money In	Money Out

DAILY PLANNER

DATE

S M T W T F S

TODAY'S GOALS

WATER INTAKE

Total :

MEAL TRACKER

Breakfast

Lunch

Dinner

Snack

MONEY TRACKER

Money In	Money Out

TODAY APPOINTMENT

Time	Event

THINGS TO GET DONE TODAY

TODAY I'M GRATEFUL FOR

SLEEP

MOOD

EXERCISE

Total Minutes

Total Steps

REMINDER

NOTES

DAILY PLANNER

DATE S M T W T F S

TODAY'S GOALS

TODAY APPOINTMENT

Time	Event

SLEEP

MOOD

WATER INTAKE

Total :

EXERCISE

Total Minutes

Total Steps

MEAL TRACKER

Breakfast

Lunch

Dinner

Snack

THINGS TO GET DONE TODAY

REMINDER

MONEY TRACKER

Money In

Money Out

TODAY I'M GRATEFUL FOR

NOTES

DAILY PLANNER

DATE

S M T W T F S

TODAY'S GOALS

TODAY APPOINTMENT

Time	Event

SLEEP

MOOD

WATER INTAKE

Total :

EXERCISE

Total Minutes

Total Steps

MEAL TRACKER

Breakfast

Lunch

Dinner

Snack

THINGS TO GET DONE TODAY

REMINDER

MONEY TRACKER

Money In	Money Out

TODAY I'M GRATEFUL FOR

NOTES

DAILY PLANNER

DATE S M T W T F S

TODAY'S GOALS

TODAY APPOINTMENT

Time	Event

SLEEP

MOOD

WATER INTAKE

Total :

EXERCISE

Total Minutes

Total Steps

THINGS TO GET DONE TODAY

MEAL TRACKER

Breakfast

Lunch

Dinner

Snack

REMINDER

TODAY I'M GRATEFUL FOR

NOTES

MONEY TRACKER

Money In	Money Out

WEEKLY PLANNER

WEEK OF

MOTIVATION

MON

TUE

WED

THUR

FRI

SAT

SUN

TO-DO

TOP PRIORITIES

NOTES

DAILY PLANNER

DATE S M T W T F S

TODAY'S GOALS

TODAY APPOINTMENT

Time	Event

SLEEP

MOOD

WATER INTAKE

Total :

EXERCISE

Total Minutes

Total Steps

THINGS TO GET DONE TODAY

MEAL TRACKER

Breakfast

Lunch

Dinner

Snack

REMINDER

TODAY I'M GRATEFUL FOR

NOTES

MONEY TRACKER

Money In	Money Out

DAILY PLANNER

DATE

S M T W T F S

TODAY'S GOALS

TODAY APPOINTMENT

Time	Event

SLEEP

MOOD

WATER INTAKE

Total :

THINGS TO GET DONE TODAY

EXERCISE

Total Minutes

Total Steps

MEAL TRACKER

Breakfast

Lunch

Dinner

Snack

REMINDER

TODAY I'M GRATEFUL FOR

NOTES

MONEY TRACKER

Money In

Money Out

DAILY PLANNER

DATE

S M T W T F S

TODAY'S GOALS

TODAY APPOINTMENT

Time	Event

SLEEP

MOOD

WATER INTAKE

Total :

EXERCISE

Total Minutes

Total Steps

MEAL TRACKER

Breakfast

Lunch

Dinner

Snack

THINGS TO GET DONE TODAY

REMINDER

MONEY TRACKER

Money In	Money Out

TODAY I'M GRATEFUL FOR

NOTES

DAILY PLANNER

DATE

S M T W T F S

TODAY'S GOALS

TODAY APPOINTMENT

Time	Event

SLEEP

MOOD

WATER INTAKE

Total :

EXERCISE

Total Minutes

Total Steps

THINGS TO GET DONE TODAY

MEAL TRACKER

Breakfast

Lunch

Dinner

Snack

REMINDER

TODAY I'M GRATEFUL FOR

MONEY TRACKER

Money In

Money Out

NOTES

DAILY PLANNER

DATE S M T W T F S

TODAY'S GOALS

TODAY APPOINTMENT

Time	Event

SLEEP

MOOD

WATER INTAKE

Total :

EXERCISE

Total Minutes

Total Steps

MEAL TRACKER

Breakfast

Lunch

Dinner

Snack

THINGS TO GET DONE TODAY

REMINDER

MONEY TRACKER

Money In

Money Out

TODAY I'M GRATEFUL FOR

NOTES

DAILY PLANNER

DATE

S M T W T F S

TODAY'S GOALS

TODAY APPOINTMENT

Time	Event

SLEEP

MOOD

WATER INTAKE

Total :

EXERCISE

Total Minutes

Total Steps

THINGS TO GET DONE TODAY

MEAL TRACKER

Breakfast

Lunch

Dinner

Snack

REMINDER

TODAY I'M GRATEFUL FOR

NOTES

MONEY TRACKER

Money In	Money Out

DAILY PLANNER

DATE S M T W T F S

TODAY'S GOALS

TODAY APPOINTMENT

Time	Event

SLEEP

MOOD

WATER INTAKE

Total :

EXERCISE

Total Minutes

Total Steps

THINGS TO GET DONE TODAY

MEAL TRACKER

Breakfast

Lunch

Dinner

Snack

REMINDER

MONEY TRACKER

Money In	Money Out

TODAY I'M GRATEFUL FOR

NOTES

NOTES

NOTES

MARCH

Monday	Tuesday	Wednesday	Thursday

To-Do

Affirmations For The month

Important Dates

Habits

To start	To stop

What do I loveabout myself?

Friday	Saturday	Sunday

Self-Care Activities

Main Goals

Appointments

Notes

MARCH BUDGET

Source Of Income	Amount
	$
	$
	$
Total Income	$

Expenses

Date	Bills	Budget	Actual
		$	$
		$	$
		$	$
		$	$
		$	$
		$	$
		$	$
		$	$
		$	$
		$	$
Total		$	$

Date	Shopping	Budget	Actual
		$	$
		$	$
		$	$
		$	$
		$	$
		$	$
Total		$	$

Date	Fees & Charges	Budget	Actual
		$	$
		$	$
		$	$
Total		$	$

Date	Groceries	Budget	Actual
		$	$
		$	$
		$	$
		$	$
		$	$
		$	$
		$	$
Total		$	$

Date	Transportation	Budget	Actual
		$	$
		$	$
		$	$
Total		$	$

Date	Entertainment	Budget	Actual
		$	$
		$	$
		$	$
Total		$	$

Date	Saving	Goal	Needed
		$	$
		$	$
		$	$
Total		$	$

TIME TRACKER

Use a green marker to highlight the hours you are focused and working on your goals. Over the course of the month – revisit and see what your productivity looks like.

DATE	AM	PM
1	1 2 3 4 5 6 7 8 9 10 11 12	1 2 3 4 5 6 7 8 9 10 11 12
2	1 2 3 4 5 6 7 8 9 10 11 12	1 2 3 4 5 6 7 8 9 10 11 12
3	1 2 3 4 5 6 7 8 9 10 11 12	1 2 3 4 5 6 7 8 9 10 11 12
4	1 2 3 4 5 6 7 8 9 10 11 12	1 2 3 4 5 6 7 8 9 10 11 12
5	1 2 3 4 5 6 7 8 9 10 11 12	1 2 3 4 5 6 7 8 9 10 11 12
6	1 2 3 4 5 6 7 8 9 10 11 12	1 2 3 4 5 6 7 8 9 10 11 12
7	1 2 3 4 5 6 7 8 9 10 11 12	1 2 3 4 5 6 7 8 9 10 11 12
8	1 2 3 4 5 6 7 8 9 10 11 12	1 2 3 4 5 6 7 8 9 10 11 12
9	1 2 3 4 5 6 7 8 9 10 11 12	1 2 3 4 5 6 7 8 9 10 11 12
10	1 2 3 4 5 6 7 8 9 10 11 12	1 2 3 4 5 6 7 8 9 10 11 12
11	1 2 3 4 5 6 7 8 9 10 11 12	1 2 3 4 5 6 7 8 9 10 11 12
12	1 2 3 4 5 6 7 8 9 10 11 12	1 2 3 4 5 6 7 8 9 10 11 12
13	1 2 3 4 5 6 7 8 9 10 11 12	1 2 3 4 5 6 7 8 9 10 11 12
14	1 2 3 4 5 6 7 8 9 10 11 12	1 2 3 4 5 6 7 8 9 10 11 12
15	1 2 3 4 5 6 7 8 9 10 11 12	1 2 3 4 5 6 7 8 9 10 11 12
16	1 2 3 4 5 6 7 8 9 10 11 12	1 2 3 4 5 6 7 8 9 10 11 12
17	1 2 3 4 5 6 7 8 9 10 11 12	1 2 3 4 5 6 7 8 9 10 11 12
18	1 2 3 4 5 6 7 8 9 10 11 12	1 2 3 4 5 6 7 8 9 10 11 12
19	1 2 3 4 5 6 7 8 9 10 11 12	1 2 3 4 5 6 7 8 9 10 11 12
20	1 2 3 4 5 6 7 8 9 10 11 12	1 2 3 4 5 6 7 8 9 10 11 12
21	1 2 3 4 5 6 7 8 9 10 11 12	1 2 3 4 5 6 7 8 9 10 11 12
22	1 2 3 4 5 6 7 8 9 10 11 12	1 2 3 4 5 6 7 8 9 10 11 12
23	1 2 3 4 5 6 7 8 9 10 11 12	1 2 3 4 5 6 7 8 9 10 11 12
24	1 2 3 4 5 6 7 8 9 10 11 12	1 2 3 4 5 6 7 8 9 10 11 12
25	1 2 3 4 5 6 7 8 9 10 11 12	1 2 3 4 5 6 7 8 9 10 11 12
26	1 2 3 4 5 6 7 8 9 10 11 12	1 2 3 4 5 6 7 8 9 10 11 12
27	1 2 3 4 5 6 7 8 9 10 11 12	1 2 3 4 5 6 7 8 9 10 11 12
28	1 2 3 4 5 6 7 8 9 10 11 12	1 2 3 4 5 6 7 8 9 10 11 12
29	1 2 3 4 5 6 7 8 9 10 11 12	1 2 3 4 5 6 7 8 9 10 11 12
30	1 2 3 4 5 6 7 8 9 10 11 12	1 2 3 4 5 6 7 8 9 10 11 12
31	1 2 3 4 5 6 7 8 9 10 11 12	1 2 3 4 5 6 7 8 9 10 11 12

CLIENT INFORMATION

Name
Phone
Email
Website
Address
Billing Adress
City
State Zip
D.O.B
Business Hours

Additional Information

Name
Phone
Email
Website
Address
Billing Adress
City
State Zip
D.O.B
Business Hours

Additional Information

Name
Phone
Email
Website
Address
Billing Adress
City
State Zip
D.O.B
Business Hours

Additional Information

Name
Phone
Email
Website
Address
Billing Adress
City
State Zip
D.O.B
Business Hours

Additional Information

CLIENT INFORMATION

Name
Phone
Email
Website
Address
Billing Adress
City
State Zip
D.O.B
Business Hours

Additional Information

Name
Phone
Email
Website
Address
Billing Adress
City
State Zip
D.O.B
Business Hours

Additional Information

Name
Phone
Email
Website
Address
Billing Adress
City
State Zip
D.O.B
Business Hours

Additional Information

Name
Phone
Email
Website
Address
Billing Adress
City
State Zip
D.O.B
Business Hours

Additional Information

MEETING NOTES

SUBJECT	DATE	TIME

AGENDA

ATTENDEES	IMPORTANT NOTES

-
-
-
-
-

SUBJECT	DATE	TIME

AGENDA

ATTENDEES	IMPORTANT NOTES

-
-
-
-
-

MEETING NOTES

SUBJECT	DATE	TIME

AGENDA

ATTENDEES	IMPORTANT NOTES
•	
•	
•	
•	
•	

SUBJECT	DATE	TIME

AGENDA

ATTENDEES	IMPORTANT NOTES
•	
•	
•	
•	
•	

MARCH SELF-CARE

Write a self-care activity and tick off each time you do self-care act.

ACTIVITIES	CHECKLIST
	1 2 3 4 5 6 7 8 9 10 11 12 13 14 15 16 17 18 19 20 21 22 23 24 25 26 27 28 29 30 31
	1 2 3 4 5 6 7 8 9 10 11 12 13 14 15 16 17 18 19 20 21 22 23 24 25 26 27 28 29 30 31
	1 2 3 4 5 6 7 8 9 10 11 12 13 14 15 16 17 18 19 20 21 22 23 24 25 26 27 28 29 30 31
	1 2 3 4 5 6 7 8 9 10 11 12 13 14 15 16 17 18 19 20 21 22 23 24 25 26 27 28 29 30 31
	1 2 3 4 5 6 7 8 9 10 11 12 13 14 15 16 17 18 19 20 21 22 23 24 25 26 27 28 29 30 31
	1 2 3 4 5 6 7 8 9 10 11 12 13 14 15 16 17 18 19 20 21 22 23 24 25 26 27 28 29 30 31
	1 2 3 4 5 6 7 8 9 10 11 12 13 14 15 16 17 18 19 20 21 22 23 24 25 26 27 28 29 30 31
	1 2 3 4 5 6 7 8 9 10 11 12 13 14 15 16 17 18 19 20 21 22 23 24 25 26 27 28 29 30 31
	1 2 3 4 5 6 7 8 9 10 11 12 13 14 15 16 17 18 19 20 21 22 23 24 25 26 27 28 29 30 31
	1 2 3 4 5 6 7 8 9 10 11 12 13 14 15 16 17 18 19 20 21 22 23 24 25 26 27 28 29 30 31

REFLECTION

HOW WILL YOU RATE THIS MONTH? ☆☆☆☆☆☆☆☆☆☆

MONTHLY WINS

-
-
-
-

HOW DOES IT MAKE ME FEEL?

-
-
-
-

CHALLENGES

-
-
-
-

HOW CAN I IMPROVE IT?

-
-
-
-

ACCOMPLISHED GOALS	UNACCOMPLISHED GOALS	GOALS NEXT MONTH

HABITS RETAINED	HABITS ELIMINATED	NEW HABITS DEVELOPED

THREE THINGS THAT I AM MOST GRATEFUL FOR THIS MONTH

1

2

3

TWO LIFE LESSONS I LEARNED THIS MONTH

1

2

ONE WORD THAT BEST DESCRIBES THIS MONTH

WEEKLY PLANNER

WEEK OF

MOTIVATION

MON

TUE

WED

THUR

FRI

SAT

SUN

TO-DO

TOP PRIORITIES

NOTES

DAILY PLANNER

DATE S M T W T F S

TODAY'S GOALS

TODAY APPOINTMENT

Time	Event

SLEEP

MOOD

WATER INTAKE

Total :

EXERCISE

Total Minutes

Total Steps

MEAL TRACKER

Breakfast

Lunch

Dinner

Snack

THINGS TO GET DONE TODAY

REMINDER

TODAY I'M GRATEFUL FOR

NOTES

MONEY TRACKER

Money In	Money Out

DAILY PLANNER

DATE

S M T W T F S

TODAY'S GOALS

TODAY APPOINTMENT

Time	Event

SLEEP

MOOD

WATER INTAKE

Total :

EXERCISE

Total Minutes

Total Steps

MEAL TRACKER

Breakfast

Lunch

Dinner

Snack

THINGS TO GET DONE TODAY

REMINDER

TODAY I'M GRATEFUL FOR

NOTES

MONEY TRACKER

Money In	Money Out

DAILY PLANNER

DATE S M T W T F S

TODAY'S GOALS

TODAY APPOINTMENT

Time	Event

SLEEP

MOOD

WATER INTAKE

Total :

EXERCISE

Total Minutes

Total Steps

THINGS TO GET DONE TODAY

MEAL TRACKER

Breakfast

Lunch

Dinner

Snack

REMINDER

TODAY I'M GRATEFUL FOR

NOTES

MONEY TRACKER

Money In	Money Out

DAILY PLANNER

DATE

S M T W T F S

TODAY'S GOALS

TODAY APPOINTMENT

Time	Event

SLEEP

MOOD

WATER INTAKE

Total :

EXERCISE

Total Minutes

Total Steps

MEAL TRACKER

Breakfast

Lunch

Dinner

Snack

THINGS TO GET DONE TODAY

REMINDER

MONEY TRACKER

Money In	Money Out

TODAY I'M GRATEFUL FOR

NOTES

DAILY PLANNER

DATE S M T W T F S

TODAY'S GOALS

TODAY APPOINTMENT

Time	Event

SLEEP

MOOD

WATER INTAKE

Total :

EXERCISE

Total Minutes

Total Steps

MEAL TRACKER

Breakfast

Lunch

Dinner

Snack

THINGS TO GET DONE TODAY

REMINDER

TODAY I'M GRATEFUL FOR

NOTES

MONEY TRACKER

Money In	Money Out

DAILY PLANNER

DATE

S M T W T F S

TODAY'S GOALS

TODAY APPOINTMENT

Time	Event

SLEEP

MOOD

WATER INTAKE

Total :

EXERCISE

Total Minutes

Total Steps

MEAL TRACKER

Breakfast

Lunch

Dinner

Snack

THINGS TO GET DONE TODAY

REMINDER

MONEY TRACKER

Money In	Money Out

TODAY I'M GRATEFUL FOR

NOTES

DAILY PLANNER

DATE S M T W T F S

TODAY'S GOALS

TODAY APPOINTMENT

Time	Event

SLEEP

MOOD

WATER INTAKE

Total :

EXERCISE

Total Minutes

Total Steps

THINGS TO GET DONE TODAY

MEAL TRACKER

Breakfast

Lunch

Dinner

Snack

REMINDER

TODAY I'M GRATEFUL FOR

MONEY TRACKER

Money In	Money Out

NOTES

WEEKLY PLANNER

WEEK OF

MOTIVATION

MON

TUE

WED

THUR

FRI

SAT

SUN

TO-DO

TOP PRIORITIES

NOTES

DAILY PLANNER

DATE S M T W T F S

TODAY'S GOALS

TODAY APPOINTMENT

Time	Event

SLEEP

MOOD

WATER INTAKE

Total :

EXERCISE

Total Minutes

Total Steps

THINGS TO GET DONE TODAY

MEAL TRACKER

Breakfast

Lunch

Dinner

Snack

REMINDER

TODAY I'M GRATEFUL FOR

NOTES

MONEY TRACKER

Money In	Money Out

DAILY PLANNER

DATE

S M T W T F S

TODAY'S GOALS

TODAY APPOINTMENT

Time	Event

SLEEP

MOOD

WATER INTAKE

Total :

EXERCISE

Total Minutes

Total Steps

MEAL TRACKER

Breakfast

Lunch

Dinner

Snack

THINGS TO GET DONE TODAY

REMINDER

TODAY I'M GRATEFUL FOR

NOTES

MONEY TRACKER

Money In	Money Out

DAILY PLANNER

DATE S M T W T F S

TODAY'S GOALS

TODAY APPOINTMENT

Time	Event

SLEEP

MOOD

WATER INTAKE

Total :

EXERCISE

Total Minutes

Total Steps

MEAL TRACKER

Breakfast

Lunch

Dinner

Snack

THINGS TO GET DONE TODAY

REMINDER

TODAY I'M GRATEFUL FOR

NOTES

MONEY TRACKER

Money In	Money Out

DAILY PLANNER

DATE

S M T W T F S

TODAY'S GOALS

TODAY APPOINTMENT

Time	Event

SLEEP

MOOD

WATER INTAKE

Total :

EXERCISE

Total Minutes

Total Steps

THINGS TO GET DONE TODAY

MEAL TRACKER

Breakfast

Lunch

Dinner

Snack

REMINDER

TODAY I'M GRATEFUL FOR

NOTES

MONEY TRACKER

Money In	Money Out

DAILY PLANNER

DATE　S M T W T F S

TODAY'S GOALS

TODAY APPOINTMENT

Time	Event

SLEEP

MOOD

WATER INTAKE

Total :

EXERCISE

Total Minutes

Total Steps

THINGS TO GET DONE TODAY

MEAL TRACKER

Breakfast

Lunch

Dinner

Snack

REMINDER

TODAY I'M GRATEFUL FOR

NOTES

MONEY TRACKER

Money In	Money Out

DAILY PLANNER

DATE

S M T W T F S

TODAY'S GOALS

TODAY APPOINTMENT

Time	Event

SLEEP

MOOD

WATER INTAKE

Total :

EXERCISE

Total Minutes

Total Steps

THINGS TO GET DONE TODAY

MEAL TRACKER

Breakfast

Lunch

Dinner

Snack

REMINDER

TODAY I'M GRATEFUL FOR

NOTES

MONEY TRACKER

Money In	Money Out

DAILY PLANNER

DATE S M T W T F S

TODAY'S GOALS

TODAY APPOINTMENT

Time	Event

SLEEP

MOOD

WATER INTAKE

Total :

EXERCISE

Total Minutes

Total Steps

MEAL TRACKER

Breakfast

Lunch

Dinner

Snack

THINGS TO GET DONE TODAY

REMINDER

MONEY TRACKER

Money In

Money Out

TODAY I'M GRATEFUL FOR

NOTES

WEEKLY PLANNER

WEEK OF

MOTIVATION

MON

TUE

WED

THUR

FRI

SAT

SUN

TO-DO

TOP PRIORITIES

NOTES

DAILY PLANNER

DATE S M T W T F S

TODAY'S GOALS

TODAY APPOINTMENT

Time	Event

SLEEP

MOOD

WATER INTAKE

Total :

EXERCISE

Total Minutes

Total Steps

MEAL TRACKER

Breakfast

Lunch

Dinner

Snack

THINGS TO GET DONE TODAY

REMINDER

TODAY I'M GRATEFUL FOR

NOTES

MONEY TRACKER

Money In	Money Out

DAILY PLANNER

DATE

S M T W T F S

TODAY'S GOALS

TODAY APPOINTMENT

Time	Event

SLEEP

MOOD

WATER INTAKE

Total :

EXERCISE

Total Minutes

Total Steps

MEAL TRACKER

Breakfast

Lunch

Dinner

Snack

THINGS TO GET DONE TODAY

REMINDER

TODAY I'M GRATEFUL FOR

NOTES

MONEY TRACKER

Money In	Money Out

DAILY PLANNER

DATE S M T W T F S

TODAY'S GOALS

TODAY APPOINTMENT

Time	Event

SLEEP

MOOD

WATER INTAKE

Total :

EXERCISE

Total Minutes

Total Steps

THINGS TO GET DONE TODAY

MEAL TRACKER

Breakfast

Lunch

Dinner

Snack

REMINDER

TODAY I'M GRATEFUL FOR

NOTES

MONEY TRACKER

Money In	Money Out

DAILY PLANNER

DATE

S M T W T F S

TODAY'S GOALS

TODAY APPOINTMENT

Time	Event

SLEEP

MOOD

WATER INTAKE

Total :

EXERCISE

Total Minutes

Total Steps

THINGS TO GET DONE TODAY

MEAL TRACKER

Breakfast

Lunch

Dinner

Snack

REMINDER

TODAY I'M GRATEFUL FOR

NOTES

MONEY TRACKER

Money In

Money Out

DAILY PLANNER

DATE S M T W T F S

TODAY'S GOALS

TODAY APPOINTMENT

Time	Event

SLEEP

MOOD

WATER INTAKE

Total :

EXERCISE

Total Minutes

Total Steps

MEAL TRACKER

Breakfast

Lunch

Dinner

Snack

THINGS TO GET DONE TODAY

REMINDER

TODAY I'M GRATEFUL FOR

NOTES

MONEY TRACKER

Money In	Money Out

DAILY PLANNER

DATE

S M T W T F S

TODAY'S GOALS

TODAY APPOINTMENT

Time	Event

SLEEP

MOOD

WATER INTAKE

Total :

EXERCISE

Total Minutes

Total Steps

THINGS TO GET DONE TODAY

MEAL TRACKER

Breakfast

Lunch

Dinner

Snack

REMINDER

TODAY I'M GRATEFUL FOR

NOTES

MONEY TRACKER

Money In	Money Out

DAILY PLANNER

DATE S M T W T F S

TODAY'S GOALS

TODAY APPOINTMENT

Time	Event

SLEEP

MOOD

WATER INTAKE

Total :

EXERCISE

Total Minutes

Total Steps

THINGS TO GET DONE TODAY

MEAL TRACKER

Breakfast

Lunch

Dinner

Snack

REMINDER

TODAY I'M GRATEFUL FOR

NOTES

MONEY TRACKER

Money In	Money Out

WEEKLY PLANNER

WEEK OF

MOTIVATION

MON

TUE

WED

THUR

FRI

SAT

SUN

TO-DO

TOP PRIORITIES

NOTES

DAILY PLANNER

DATE S M T W T F S

TODAY'S GOALS

TODAY APPOINTMENT

Time	Event

SLEEP

MOOD

WATER INTAKE

Total :

EXERCISE

Total Minutes

Total Steps

MEAL TRACKER

Breakfast

Lunch

Dinner

Snack

THINGS TO GET DONE TODAY

REMINDER

MONEY TRACKER

Money In

Money Out

TODAY I'M GRATEFUL FOR

NOTES

DAILY PLANNER

DATE

S M T W T F S

TODAY'S GOALS

TODAY APPOINTMENT

Time	Event

SLEEP

MOOD

WATER INTAKE

Total :

EXERCISE

Total Minutes

Total Steps

THINGS TO GET DONE TODAY

MEAL TRACKER

Breakfast

Lunch

Dinner

Snack

REMINDER

TODAY I'M GRATEFUL FOR

NOTES

MONEY TRACKER

Money In	Money Out

DAILY PLANNER

DATE S M T W T F S

TODAY'S GOALS

TODAY APPOINTMENT

Time	Event

SLEEP

MOOD

WATER INTAKE

Total :

EXERCISE

Total Minutes

Total Steps

THINGS TO GET DONE TODAY

MEAL TRACKER

Breakfast

Lunch

Dinner

Snack

REMINDER

TODAY I'M GRATEFUL FOR

NOTES

MONEY TRACKER

Money In	Money Out

DAILY PLANNER

DATE

S M T W T F S

TODAY'S GOALS

TODAY APPOINTMENT

Time	Event

SLEEP

MOOD

WATER INTAKE

Total :

EXERCISE

Total Minutes

Total Steps

MEAL TRACKER

Breakfast

Lunch

Dinner

Snack

THINGS TO GET DONE TODAY

REMINDER

TODAY I'M GRATEFUL FOR

NOTES

MONEY TRACKER

Money In	Money Out

DAILY PLANNER

DATE S M T W T F S

TODAY'S GOALS

TODAY APPOINTMENT

Time	Event

SLEEP

MOOD

WATER INTAKE

Total :

EXERCISE

Total Minutes

Total Steps

THINGS TO GET DONE TODAY

MEAL TRACKER

Breakfast

Lunch

Dinner

Snack

REMINDER

TODAY I'M GRATEFUL FOR

NOTES

MONEY TRACKER

Money In	Money Out

DAILY PLANNER

DATE

S M T W T F S

TODAY'S GOALS

TODAY APPOINTMENT

Time	Event

SLEEP

MOOD

WATER INTAKE

Total :

EXERCISE

Total Minutes

Total Steps

THINGS TO GET DONE TODAY

MEAL TRACKER

Breakfast

Lunch

Dinner

Snack

REMINDER

TODAY I'M GRATEFUL FOR

NOTES

MONEY TRACKER

Money In	Money Out

DAILY PLANNER

DATE S M T W T F S

TODAY'S GOALS

TODAY APPOINTMENT

Time	Event

SLEEP

MOOD

WATER INTAKE

Total :

EXERCISE

Total Minutes

Total Steps

MEAL TRACKER

Breakfast

Lunch

Dinner

Snack

THINGS TO GET DONE TODAY

REMINDER

TODAY I'M GRATEFUL FOR

NOTES

MONEY TRACKER

Money In	Money Out

DAILY PLANNER

DATE

S M T W T F S

TODAY'S GOALS

TODAY APPOINTMENT

Time	Event

SLEEP

MOOD

WATER INTAKE

Total :

EXERCISE

Total Minutes

Total Steps

THINGS TO GET DONE TODAY

MEAL TRACKER

Breakfast

Lunch

Dinner

Snack

REMINDER

TODAY I'M GRATEFUL FOR

NOTES

MONEY TRACKER

Money In	Money Out

DAILY PLANNER

DATE S M T W T F S

TODAY'S GOALS

TODAY APPOINTMENT

Time	Event

SLEEP

MOOD

WATER INTAKE

Total :

EXERCISE

Total Minutes

Total Steps

THINGS TO GET DONE TODAY

MEAL TRACKER

Breakfast

Lunch

Dinner

Snack

REMINDER

TODAY I'M GRATEFUL FOR

NOTES

MONEY TRACKER

Money In	Money Out

DAILY PLANNER

DATE

S M T W T F S

TODAY'S GOALS

TODAY APPOINTMENT

Time	Event

SLEEP

MOOD

WATER INTAKE

Total :

EXERCISE

Total Minutes

Total Steps

THINGS TO GET DONE TODAY

MEAL TRACKER

Breakfast

Lunch

Dinner

Snack

REMINDER

TODAY I'M GRATEFUL FOR

NOTES

MONEY TRACKER

Money In	Money Out

NOTES

APRIL

Monday	Tuesday	Wednesday	Thursday

To-Do

Affirmations For The month

Important Dates

Habits

To start	To stop

What do I love about myself?

Friday	Saturday	Sunday

Self-Care Activities

Main Goals

Appointments

Notes

APRIL BUDGET

Source Of Income	Amount
	$
	$
	$
Total Income	$

Expenses

Date	Bills	Budget	Actual
		$	$
		$	$
		$	$
		$	$
		$	$
		$	$
		$	$
		$	$
		$	$
		$	$
Total		$	$

Date	Groceries	Budget	Actual
		$	$
		$	$
		$	$
		$	$
		$	$
		$	$
		$	$
Total		$	$

Date	Transportation	Budget	Actual
		$	$
		$	$
		$	$
Total		$	$

Date	Shopping	Budget	Actual
		$	$
		$	$
		$	$
		$	$
		$	$
		$	$
Total		$	$

Date	Entertainment	Budget	Actual
		$	$
		$	$
		$	$
Total		$	$

Date	Fees & Charges	Budget	Actual
		$	$
		$	$
		$	$
Total		$	$

Date	Saving	Goal	Needed
		$	$
		$	$
		$	$
Total		$	$

TIME TRACKER

Use a green marker to highlight the hours you are focused and working on your goals. Over the course of the month – revisit and see what your productivity looks like.

DATE	AM	PM
1	1 2 3 4 5 6 7 8 9 10 11 12	1 2 3 4 5 6 7 8 9 10 11 12
2	1 2 3 4 5 6 7 8 9 10 11 12	1 2 3 4 5 6 7 8 9 10 11 12
3	1 2 3 4 5 6 7 8 9 10 11 12	1 2 3 4 5 6 7 8 9 10 11 12
4	1 2 3 4 5 6 7 8 9 10 11 12	1 2 3 4 5 6 7 8 9 10 11 12
5	1 2 3 4 5 6 7 8 9 10 11 12	1 2 3 4 5 6 7 8 9 10 11 12
6	1 2 3 4 5 6 7 8 9 10 11 12	1 2 3 4 5 6 7 8 9 10 11 12
7	1 2 3 4 5 6 7 8 9 10 11 12	1 2 3 4 5 6 7 8 9 10 11 12
8	1 2 3 4 5 6 7 8 9 10 11 12	1 2 3 4 5 6 7 8 9 10 11 12
9	1 2 3 4 5 6 7 8 9 10 11 12	1 2 3 4 5 6 7 8 9 10 11 12
10	1 2 3 4 5 6 7 8 9 10 11 12	1 2 3 4 5 6 7 8 9 10 11 12
11	1 2 3 4 5 6 7 8 9 10 11 12	1 2 3 4 5 6 7 8 9 10 11 12
12	1 2 3 4 5 6 7 8 9 10 11 12	1 2 3 4 5 6 7 8 9 10 11 12
13	1 2 3 4 5 6 7 8 9 10 11 12	1 2 3 4 5 6 7 8 9 10 11 12
14	1 2 3 4 5 6 7 8 9 10 11 12	1 2 3 4 5 6 7 8 9 10 11 12
15	1 2 3 4 5 6 7 8 9 10 11 12	1 2 3 4 5 6 7 8 9 10 11 12
16	1 2 3 4 5 6 7 8 9 10 11 12	1 2 3 4 5 6 7 8 9 10 11 12
17	1 2 3 4 5 6 7 8 9 10 11 12	1 2 3 4 5 6 7 8 9 10 11 12
18	1 2 3 4 5 6 7 8 9 10 11 12	1 2 3 4 5 6 7 8 9 10 11 12
19	1 2 3 4 5 6 7 8 9 10 11 12	1 2 3 4 5 6 7 8 9 10 11 12
20	1 2 3 4 5 6 7 8 9 10 11 12	1 2 3 4 5 6 7 8 9 10 11 12
21	1 2 3 4 5 6 7 8 9 10 11 12	1 2 3 4 5 6 7 8 9 10 11 12
22	1 2 3 4 5 6 7 8 9 10 11 12	1 2 3 4 5 6 7 8 9 10 11 12
23	1 2 3 4 5 6 7 8 9 10 11 12	1 2 3 4 5 6 7 8 9 10 11 12
24	1 2 3 4 5 6 7 8 9 10 11 12	1 2 3 4 5 6 7 8 9 10 11 12
25	1 2 3 4 5 6 7 8 9 10 11 12	1 2 3 4 5 6 7 8 9 10 11 12
26	1 2 3 4 5 6 7 8 9 10 11 12	1 2 3 4 5 6 7 8 9 10 11 12
27	1 2 3 4 5 6 7 8 9 10 11 12	1 2 3 4 5 6 7 8 9 10 11 12
28	1 2 3 4 5 6 7 8 9 10 11 12	1 2 3 4 5 6 7 8 9 10 11 12
29	1 2 3 4 5 6 7 8 9 10 11 12	1 2 3 4 5 6 7 8 9 10 11 12
30	1 2 3 4 5 6 7 8 9 10 11 12	1 2 3 4 5 6 7 8 9 10 11 12
31	1 2 3 4 5 6 7 8 9 10 11 12	1 2 3 4 5 6 7 8 9 10 11 12

CLIENT INFORMATION

Name
Phone
Email
Website
Address
Billing Adress
City
State Zip
D.O.B
Business Hours

Additional Information

Name
Phone
Email
Website
Address
Billing Adress
City
State Zip
D.O.B
Business Hours

Additional Information

Name
Phone
Email
Website
Address
Billing Adress
City
State Zip
D.O.B
Business Hours

Additional Information

Name
Phone
Email
Website
Address
Billing Adress
City
State Zip
D.O.B
Business Hours

Additional Information

CLIENT INFORMATION

Name
Phone
Email
Website
Address
Billing Adress
City
State Zip
D.O.B
Business Hours

Additional Information

Name
Phone
Email
Website
Address
Billing Adress
City
State Zip
D.O.B
Business Hours

Additional Information

Name
Phone
Email
Website
Address
Billing Adress
City
State Zip
D.O.B
Business Hours

Additional Information

Name
Phone
Email
Website
Address
Billing Adress
City
State Zip
D.O.B
Business Hours

Additional Information

MEETING NOTES

SUBJECT	DATE	TIME

AGENDA

ATTENDEES

IMPORTANT NOTES

SUBJECT	DATE	TIME

AGENDA

ATTENDEES

IMPORTANT NOTES

MEETING NOTES

SUBJECT	DATE	TIME

AGENDA

ATTENDEES

-
-
-
-
-

IMPORTANT NOTES

SUBJECT	DATE	TIME

AGENDA

ATTENDEES

-
-
-
-
-

IMPORTANT NOTES

APRIL SELF-CARE

Write a self-care activity and tick off each time you do self-care act.

ACTIVITIES	CHECKLIST
	1 2 3 4 5 6 7 8 9 10 11 12 13 14 15 16 17 18 19 20 21 22 23 24 25 26 27 28 29 30 31
	1 2 3 4 5 6 7 8 9 10 11 12 13 14 15 16 17 18 19 20 21 22 23 24 25 26 27 28 29 30 31
	1 2 3 4 5 6 7 8 9 10 11 12 13 14 15 16 17 18 19 20 21 22 23 24 25 26 27 28 29 30 31
	1 2 3 4 5 6 7 8 9 10 11 12 13 14 15 16 17 18 19 20 21 22 23 24 25 26 27 28 29 30 31
	1 2 3 4 5 6 7 8 9 10 11 12 13 14 15 16 17 18 19 20 21 22 23 24 25 26 27 28 29 30 31
	1 2 3 4 5 6 7 8 9 10 11 12 13 14 15 16 17 18 19 20 21 22 23 24 25 26 27 28 29 30 31
	1 2 3 4 5 6 7 8 9 10 11 12 13 14 15 16 17 18 19 20 21 22 23 24 25 26 27 28 29 30 31
	1 2 3 4 5 6 7 8 9 10 11 12 13 14 15 16 17 18 19 20 21 22 23 24 25 26 27 28 29 30 31
	1 2 3 4 5 6 7 8 9 10 11 12 13 14 15 16 17 18 19 20 21 22 23 24 25 26 27 28 29 30 31
	1 2 3 4 5 6 7 8 9 10 11 12 13 14 15 16 17 18 19 20 21 22 23 24 25 26 27 28 29 30 31

REFLECTION

HOW WILL YOU RATE THIS MONTH? ☆ ☆ ☆ ☆ ☆ ☆ ☆ ☆ ☆ ☆

MONTHLY WINS

HOW DOES IT MAKE ME FEEL?

CHALLENGES

HOW CAN I IMPROVE IT?

ACCOMPLISHED GOALS

UNACCOMPLISHED GOALS

GOALS NEXT MONTH

HABITS RETAINED

HABITS ELIMINATED

NEW HABITS DEVELOPED

THREE THINGS THAT I AM MOST GRATEFUL FOR THIS MONTH

1

2

3

TWO LIFE LESSONS I LEARNED THIS MONTH

1

2

ONE WORD THAT BEST DESCRIBES THIS MONTH

WEEKLY PLANNER

WEEK OF

MOTIVATION

MON

TUE

WED

THUR

FRI

SAT

SUN

TO-DO

TOP PRIORITIES

NOTES

DAILY PLANNER

DATE S M T W T F S

TODAY'S GOALS

TODAY APPOINTMENT

Time	Event

SLEEP

MOOD

WATER INTAKE

Total :

EXERCISE

Total Minutes

Total Steps

MEAL TRACKER

Breakfast

Lunch

Dinner

Snack

THINGS TO GET DONE TODAY

REMINDER

TODAY I'M GRATEFUL FOR

NOTES

MONEY TRACKER

Money In	Money Out

DAILY PLANNER

DATE

S M T W T F S

TODAY'S GOALS

TODAY APPOINTMENT

Time	Event

SLEEP

MOOD

WATER INTAKE

Total :

THINGS TO GET DONE TODAY

EXERCISE

Total Minutes

Total Steps

MEAL TRACKER

Breakfast

Lunch

Dinner

Snack

REMINDER

TODAY I'M GRATEFUL FOR

NOTES

MONEY TRACKER

Money In	Money Out

DAILY PLANNER

DATE S M T W T F S

TODAY'S GOALS

TODAY APPOINTMENT

Time	Event

SLEEP

MOOD

WATER INTAKE

Total :

EXERCISE

Total Minutes

Total Steps

MEAL TRACKER

Breakfast

Lunch

Dinner

Snack

THINGS TO GET DONE TODAY

REMINDER

MONEY TRACKER

Money In	Money Out

TODAY I'M GRATEFUL FOR

NOTES

DAILY PLANNER

DATE

S M T W T F S

TODAY'S GOALS

TODAY APPOINTMENT

Time	Event

SLEEP

MOOD

WATER INTAKE

Total :

EXERCISE

Total Minutes

Total Steps

THINGS TO GET DONE TODAY

MEAL TRACKER

Breakfast

Lunch

Dinner

Snack

REMINDER

TODAY I'M GRATEFUL FOR

NOTES

MONEY TRACKER

Money In	Money Out

DAILY PLANNER

DATE S M T W T F S

TODAY'S GOALS

TODAY APPOINTMENT

Time	Event

SLEEP

MOOD

WATER INTAKE

Total :

EXERCISE

Total Minutes

Total Steps

MEAL TRACKER

Breakfast

Lunch

Dinner

Snack

THINGS TO GET DONE TODAY

REMINDER

MONEY TRACKER

Money In	Money Out

TODAY I'M GRATEFUL FOR

NOTES

DAILY PLANNER

DATE

S M T W T F S

TODAY'S GOALS

TODAY APPOINTMENT

Time	Event

SLEEP

MOOD

WATER INTAKE

Total :

EXERCISE

Total Minutes

Total Steps

THINGS TO GET DONE TODAY

MEAL TRACKER

Breakfast

Lunch

Dinner

Snack

REMINDER

TODAY I'M GRATEFUL FOR

NOTES

MONEY TRACKER

Money In	Money Out

DAILY PLANNER

DATE S M T W T F S

TODAY'S GOALS

TODAY APPOINTMENT

Time	Event

SLEEP

MOOD

WATER INTAKE

Total :

EXERCISE

Total Minutes

Total Steps

MEAL TRACKER

Breakfast

Lunch

Dinner

Snack

THINGS TO GET DONE TODAY

REMINDER

TODAY I'M GRATEFUL FOR

NOTES

MONEY TRACKER

Money In	Money Out

WEEKLY PLANNER

WEEK OF	
MOTIVATION	

MON	
TUE	
WED	
THUR	
FRI	
SAT	
SUN	

TO-DO

- ○
- ○
- ○
- ○
- ○
- ○

TOP PRIORITIES

- ○
- ○
- ○
- ○

NOTES

DAILY PLANNER

DATE S M T W T F S

TODAY'S GOALS

TODAY APPOINTMENT

Time	Event

SLEEP

MOOD

WATER INTAKE

Total :

EXERCISE

Total Minutes

Total Steps

MEAL TRACKER

Breakfast

Lunch

Dinner

Snack

THINGS TO GET DONE TODAY

REMINDER

TODAY I'M GRATEFUL FOR

NOTES

MONEY TRACKER

Money In	Money Out

DAILY PLANNER

DATE

S M T W T F S

TODAY'S GOALS

TODAY APPOINTMENT

Time	Event

SLEEP

MOOD

WATER INTAKE

Total :

THINGS TO GET DONE TODAY

EXERCISE

Total Minutes

Total Steps

MEAL TRACKER

Breakfast

Lunch

Dinner

Snack

REMINDER

TODAY I'M GRATEFUL FOR

NOTES

MONEY TRACKER

Money In	Money Out

DAILY PLANNER

DATE S M T W T F S

TODAY'S GOALS

TODAY APPOINTMENT

Time	Event

SLEEP

MOOD

WATER INTAKE

Total :

EXERCISE

Total Minutes

Total Steps

MEAL TRACKER

Breakfast

Lunch

Dinner

Snack

THINGS TO GET DONE TODAY

REMINDER

TODAY I'M GRATEFUL FOR

NOTES

MONEY TRACKER

Money In	Money Out

DAILY PLANNER

DATE

S M T W T F S

TODAY'S GOALS

TODAY APPOINTMENT

Time	Event

SLEEP

MOOD

WATER INTAKE

Total :

EXERCISE

Total Minutes

Total Steps

MEAL TRACKER

Breakfast

Lunch

Dinner

Snack

THINGS TO GET DONE TODAY

REMINDER

MONEY TRACKER

Money In

Money Out

TODAY I'M GRATEFUL FOR

NOTES

DAILY PLANNER

DATE S M T W T F S

TODAY'S GOALS

TODAY APPOINTMENT

Time	Event

SLEEP

MOOD

WATER INTAKE

Total :

EXERCISE

Total Minutes

Total Steps

MEAL TRACKER

Breakfast

Lunch

Dinner

Snack

THINGS TO GET DONE TODAY

REMINDER

MONEY TRACKER

Money In	Money Out

TODAY I'M GRATEFUL FOR

NOTES

DAILY PLANNER

DATE

S M T W T F S

TODAY'S GOALS

TODAY APPOINTMENT

Time	Event

SLEEP

MOOD

WATER INTAKE

Total :

EXERCISE

Total Minutes

Total Steps

THINGS TO GET DONE TODAY

MEAL TRACKER

Breakfast

Lunch

Dinner

Snack

REMINDER

TODAY I'M GRATEFUL FOR

MONEY TRACKER

Money In	Money Out

NOTES

DAILY PLANNER

DATE

S M T W T F S

TODAY'S GOALS

TODAY APPOINTMENT

Time	Event

SLEEP

MOOD

WATER INTAKE

Total :

EXERCISE

Total Minutes

Total Steps

MEAL TRACKER

Breakfast

Lunch

Dinner

Snack

THINGS TO GET DONE TODAY

REMINDER

MONEY TRACKER

Money In

Money Out

TODAY I'M GRATEFUL FOR

NOTES

WEEKLY PLANNER

WEEK OF

MOTIVATION

MON

TUE

WED

THUR

FRI

SAT

SUN

TO-DO

TOP PRIORITIES

NOTES

DAILY PLANNER

DATE S M T W T F S

TODAY'S GOALS

TODAY APPOINTMENT

Time	Event

SLEEP

MOOD

WATER INTAKE

Total :

EXERCISE

Total Minutes

Total Steps

THINGS TO GET DONE TODAY

MEAL TRACKER

Breakfast

Lunch

Dinner

Snack

REMINDER

TODAY I'M GRATEFUL FOR

NOTES

MONEY TRACKER

Money In	Money Out

DAILY PLANNER

DATE

S M T W T F S

TODAY'S GOALS

TODAY APPOINTMENT

Time	Event

SLEEP

MOOD

WATER INTAKE

Total :

EXERCISE

Total Minutes

Total Steps

MEAL TRACKER

Breakfast

Lunch

Dinner

Snack

THINGS TO GET DONE TODAY

REMINDER

TODAY I'M GRATEFUL FOR

NOTES

MONEY TRACKER

Money In	Money Out

DAILY PLANNER

DATE S M T W T F S

TODAY'S GOALS

TODAY APPOINTMENT

Time	Event

SLEEP

MOOD

WATER INTAKE

Total :

EXERCISE

Total Minutes

Total Steps

MEAL TRACKER

Breakfast

Lunch

Dinner

Snack

THINGS TO GET DONE TODAY

REMINDER

MONEY TRACKER

Money In	Money Out

TODAY I'M GRATEFUL FOR

NOTES

DAILY PLANNER

DATE

S M T W T F S

TODAY'S GOALS

TODAY APPOINTMENT

Time	Event

SLEEP

MOOD

WATER INTAKE

Total :

EXERCISE

Total Minutes

Total Steps

THINGS TO GET DONE TODAY

MEAL TRACKER

Breakfast

Lunch

Dinner

Snack

REMINDER

TODAY I'M GRATEFUL FOR

NOTES

MONEY TRACKER

Money In	Money Out

DAILY PLANNER

DATE S M T W T F S

TODAY'S GOALS

TODAY APPOINTMENT

Time	Event

SLEEP

MOOD

WATER INTAKE

Total :

EXERCISE

Total Minutes

Total Steps

MEAL TRACKER

Breakfast

Lunch

Dinner

Snack

THINGS TO GET DONE TODAY

REMINDER

MONEY TRACKER

Money In

Money Out

TODAY I'M GRATEFUL FOR

NOTES

DAILY PLANNER

DATE

S M T W T F S

TODAY'S GOALS

TODAY APPOINTMENT

Time	Event

SLEEP

MOOD

WATER INTAKE

Total :

EXERCISE

Total Minutes

Total Steps

THINGS TO GET DONE TODAY

MEAL TRACKER

Breakfast

Lunch

Dinner

Snack

REMINDER

TODAY I'M GRATEFUL FOR

NOTES

MONEY TRACKER

Money In	Money Out

DAILY PLANNER

DATE S M T W T F S

TODAY'S GOALS

TODAY APPOINTMENT

Time	Event

SLEEP

MOOD

WATER INTAKE

Total :

EXERCISE

Total Minutes

Total Steps

MEAL TRACKER

Breakfast

Lunch

Dinner

Snack

THINGS TO GET DONE TODAY

REMINDER

MONEY TRACKER

Money In

Money Out

TODAY I'M GRATEFUL FOR

NOTES

WEEKLY PLANNER

WEEK OF

MOTIVATION

MON

TUE

WED

THUR

FRI

SAT

SUN

TO-DO

TOP PRIORITIES

NOTES

DAILY PLANNER

DATE S M T W T F S

TODAY'S GOALS

TODAY APPOINTMENT

Time	Event

SLEEP

MOOD

WATER INTAKE

Total :

EXERCISE

Total Minutes

Total Steps

MEAL TRACKER

Breakfast

Lunch

Dinner

Snack

THINGS TO GET DONE TODAY

REMINDER

TODAY I'M GRATEFUL FOR

NOTES

MONEY TRACKER

Money In	Money Out

DAILY PLANNER

DATE

S M T W T F S

TODAY'S GOALS

TODAY APPOINTMENT

Time	Event

SLEEP

MOOD

WATER INTAKE

Total :

EXERCISE

Total Minutes

Total Steps

MEAL TRACKER

Breakfast

Lunch

Dinner

Snack

THINGS TO GET DONE TODAY

REMINDER

MONEY TRACKER

Money In	Money Out

TODAY I'M GRATEFUL FOR

NOTES

DAILY PLANNER

DATE S M T W T F S

TODAY'S GOALS

TODAY APPOINTMENT

Time	Event

SLEEP

MOOD

WATER INTAKE

Total :

EXERCISE

Total Minutes

Total Steps

MEAL TRACKER

Breakfast

Lunch

Dinner

Snack

THINGS TO GET DONE TODAY

REMINDER

MONEY TRACKER

Money In	Money Out

TODAY I'M GRATEFUL FOR

NOTES

DAILY PLANNER

DATE

S M T W T F S

TODAY'S GOALS

TODAY APPOINTMENT

Time	Event

SLEEP

MOOD

WATER INTAKE

Total :

EXERCISE

Total Minutes

Total Steps

THINGS TO GET DONE TODAY

MEAL TRACKER

Breakfast

Lunch

Dinner

Snack

REMINDER

TODAY I'M GRATEFUL FOR

NOTES

MONEY TRACKER

Money In	Money Out

DAILY PLANNER

DATE S M T W T F S

TODAY'S GOALS

TODAY APPOINTMENT

Time	Event

SLEEP

MOOD

WATER INTAKE

Total :

EXERCISE

Total Minutes

Total Steps

THINGS TO GET DONE TODAY

MEAL TRACKER

Breakfast

Lunch

Dinner

Snack

REMINDER

TODAY I'M GRATEFUL FOR

NOTES

MONEY TRACKER

Money In	Money Out

DAILY PLANNER

DATE

S M T W T F S

TODAY'S GOALS

TODAY APPOINTMENT

Time	Event

SLEEP

MOOD

WATER INTAKE

Total :

EXERCISE

Total Minutes

Total Steps

THINGS TO GET DONE TODAY

MEAL TRACKER

Breakfast

Lunch

Dinner

Snack

REMINDER

TODAY I'M GRATEFUL FOR

NOTES

MONEY TRACKER

Money In	Money Out

DAILY PLANNER

DATE S M T W T F S

TODAY'S GOALS

TODAY APPOINTMENT

Time	Event

SLEEP

MOOD

WATER INTAKE

Total :

EXERCISE

Total Minutes

Total Steps

MEAL TRACKER

Breakfast

Lunch

Dinner

Snack

THINGS TO GET DONE TODAY

REMINDER

MONEY TRACKER

Money In	Money Out

TODAY I'M GRATEFUL FOR

NOTES

DAILY PLANNER

DATE

S M T W T F S

TODAY'S GOALS

TODAY APPOINTMENT

Time	Event

SLEEP

MOOD

WATER INTAKE

Total :

EXERCISE

Total Minutes

Total Steps

MEAL TRACKER

Breakfast

Lunch

Dinner

Snack

THINGS TO GET DONE TODAY

REMINDER

MONEY TRACKER

Money In	Money Out

TODAY I'M GRATEFUL FOR

NOTES

DAILY PLANNER

DATE S M T W T F S

TODAY'S GOALS

TODAY APPOINTMENT

Time	Event

SLEEP

MOOD

WATER INTAKE

Total :

EXERCISE

Total Minutes

Total Steps

MEAL TRACKER

Breakfast

Lunch

Dinner

Snack

THINGS TO GET DONE TODAY

REMINDER

MONEY TRACKER

Money In	Money Out

TODAY I'M GRATEFUL FOR

NOTES

NOTES

NOTES

MAY

To-Do

Monday	Tuesday	Wednesday	Thursday

Affirmations For The month

Important Dates

Habits

To start	To stop

What do I loveabout myself?

Friday	Saturday	Sunday

Self-Care Activities

Main Goals

Appointments

Notes

MAY BUDGET

Source Of Income	Amount
	$
	$
	$
Total Income	$

Expenses

Date	Bills	Budget	Actual
		$	$
		$	$
		$	$
		$	$
		$	$
		$	$
		$	$
		$	$
		$	$
		$	$
Total		$	$

Date	Groceries	Budget	Actual
		$	$
		$	$
		$	$
		$	$
		$	$
		$	$
		$	$
Total		$	$

Date	Trasnportation	Budget	Actual
		$	$
		$	$
		$	$
Total		$	$

Date	Shopping	Budget	Actual
		$	$
		$	$
		$	$
		$	$
		$	$
		$	$
Total		$	$

Date	Entertainment	Budget	Actual
		$	$
		$	$
		$	$
Total		$	$

Date	Fees & Charges	Budget	Actual
		$	$
		$	$
		$	$
Total		$	$

Date	Saving	Goal	Needed
		$	$
		$	$
		$	$
Total		$	$

TIME TRACKER

Use a green marker to highlight the hours you are focused and working on your goals. Over the course of the month – revisit and see what your productivity looks like.

DATE	AM	PM
1	1 2 3 4 5 6 7 8 9 10 11 12	1 2 3 4 5 6 7 8 9 10 11 12
2	1 2 3 4 5 6 7 8 9 10 11 12	1 2 3 4 5 6 7 8 9 10 11 12
3	1 2 3 4 5 6 7 8 9 10 11 12	1 2 3 4 5 6 7 8 9 10 11 12
4	1 2 3 4 5 6 7 8 9 10 11 12	1 2 3 4 5 6 7 8 9 10 11 12
5	1 2 3 4 5 6 7 8 9 10 11 12	1 2 3 4 5 6 7 8 9 10 11 12
6	1 2 3 4 5 6 7 8 9 10 11 12	1 2 3 4 5 6 7 8 9 10 11 12
7	1 2 3 4 5 6 7 8 9 10 11 12	1 2 3 4 5 6 7 8 9 10 11 12
8	1 2 3 4 5 6 7 8 9 10 11 12	1 2 3 4 5 6 7 8 9 10 11 12
9	1 2 3 4 5 6 7 8 9 10 11 12	1 2 3 4 5 6 7 8 9 10 11 12
10	1 2 3 4 5 6 7 8 9 10 11 12	1 2 3 4 5 6 7 8 9 10 11 12
11	1 2 3 4 5 6 7 8 9 10 11 12	1 2 3 4 5 6 7 8 9 10 11 12
12	1 2 3 4 5 6 7 8 9 10 11 12	1 2 3 4 5 6 7 8 9 10 11 12
13	1 2 3 4 5 6 7 8 9 10 11 12	1 2 3 4 5 6 7 8 9 10 11 12
14	1 2 3 4 5 6 7 8 9 10 11 12	1 2 3 4 5 6 7 8 9 10 11 12
15	1 2 3 4 5 6 7 8 9 10 11 12	1 2 3 4 5 6 7 8 9 10 11 12
16	1 2 3 4 5 6 7 8 9 10 11 12	1 2 3 4 5 6 7 8 9 10 11 12
17	1 2 3 4 5 6 7 8 9 10 11 12	1 2 3 4 5 6 7 8 9 10 11 12
18	1 2 3 4 5 6 7 8 9 10 11 12	1 2 3 4 5 6 7 8 9 10 11 12
19	1 2 3 4 5 6 7 8 9 10 11 12	1 2 3 4 5 6 7 8 9 10 11 12
20	1 2 3 4 5 6 7 8 9 10 11 12	1 2 3 4 5 6 7 8 9 10 11 12
21	1 2 3 4 5 6 7 8 9 10 11 12	1 2 3 4 5 6 7 8 9 10 11 12
22	1 2 3 4 5 6 7 8 9 10 11 12	1 2 3 4 5 6 7 8 9 10 11 12
23	1 2 3 4 5 6 7 8 9 10 11 12	1 2 3 4 5 6 7 8 9 10 11 12
24	1 2 3 4 5 6 7 8 9 10 11 12	1 2 3 4 5 6 7 8 9 10 11 12
25	1 2 3 4 5 6 7 8 9 10 11 12	1 2 3 4 5 6 7 8 9 10 11 12
26	1 2 3 4 5 6 7 8 9 10 11 12	1 2 3 4 5 6 7 8 9 10 11 12
27	1 2 3 4 5 6 7 8 9 10 11 12	1 2 3 4 5 6 7 8 9 10 11 12
28	1 2 3 4 5 6 7 8 9 10 11 12	1 2 3 4 5 6 7 8 9 10 11 12
29	1 2 3 4 5 6 7 8 9 10 11 12	1 2 3 4 5 6 7 8 9 10 11 12
30	1 2 3 4 5 6 7 8 9 10 11 12	1 2 3 4 5 6 7 8 9 10 11 12
31	1 2 3 4 5 6 7 8 9 10 11 12	1 2 3 4 5 6 7 8 9 10 11 12

CLIENT INFORMATION

Name
Phone
Email
Website
Address
Billing Adress
City
State Zip
D.O.B
Business Hours

Additional Information

Name
Phone
Email
Website
Address
Billing Adress
City
State Zip
D.O.B
Business Hours

Additional Information

Name
Phone
Email
Website
Address
Billing Adress
City
State Zip
D.O.B
Business Hours

Additional Information

Name
Phone
Email
Website
Address
Billing Adress
City
State Zip
D.O.B
Business Hours

Additional Information

CLIENT INFORMATION

Name
Phone
Email
Website
Address
Billing Adress
City
State Zip
D.O.B
Business Hours

Additional Information

Name
Phone
Email
Website
Address
Billing Adress
City
State Zip
D.O.B
Business Hours

Additional Information

Name
Phone
Email
Website
Address
Billing Adress
City
State Zip
D.O.B
Business Hours

Additional Information

Name
Phone
Email
Website
Address
Billing Adress
City
State Zip
D.O.B
Business Hours

Additional Information

MEETING NOTES

SUBJECT	DATE	TIME

AGENDA

ATTENDEES

-
-
-
-
-

IMPORTANT NOTES

SUBJECT	DATE	TIME

AGENDA

ATTENDEES

-
-
-
-
-

IMPORTANT NOTES

MEETING NOTES

SUBJECT	DATE	TIME

AGENDA

ATTENDEES

IMPORTANT NOTES

SUBJECT	DATE	TIME

AGENDA

ATTENDEES

IMPORTANT NOTES

MAY SELF-CARE

Write a self-care activity and tick off each time you do self-care act.

ACTIVITIES	CHECKLIST
	1 2 3 4 5 6 7 8 9 10 11 12 13 14 15 16 17 18 19 20 21 22 23 24 25 26 27 28 29 30 31
	1 2 3 4 5 6 7 8 9 10 11 12 13 14 15 16 17 18 19 20 21 22 23 24 25 26 27 28 29 30 31
	1 2 3 4 5 6 7 8 9 10 11 12 13 14 15 16 17 18 19 20 21 22 23 24 25 26 27 28 29 30 31
	1 2 3 4 5 6 7 8 9 10 11 12 13 14 15 16 17 18 19 20 21 22 23 24 25 26 27 28 29 30 31
	1 2 3 4 5 6 7 8 9 10 11 12 13 14 15 16 17 18 19 20 21 22 23 24 25 26 27 28 29 30 31
	1 2 3 4 5 6 7 8 9 10 11 12 13 14 15 16 17 18 19 20 21 22 23 24 25 26 27 28 29 30 31
	1 2 3 4 5 6 7 8 9 10 11 12 13 14 15 16 17 18 19 20 21 22 23 24 25 26 27 28 29 30 31
	1 2 3 4 5 6 7 8 9 10 11 12 13 14 15 16 17 18 19 20 21 22 23 24 25 26 27 28 29 30 31
	1 2 3 4 5 6 7 8 9 10 11 12 13 14 15 16 17 18 19 20 21 22 23 24 25 26 27 28 29 30 31
	1 2 3 4 5 6 7 8 9 10 11 12 13 14 15 16 17 18 19 20 21 22 23 24 25 26 27 28 29 30 31

REFLECTION

HOW WILL YOU RATE THIS MONTH? ☆ ☆ ☆ ☆ ☆ ☆ ☆ ☆ ☆ ☆

MONTHLY WINS

-
-
-
-

HOW DOES IT MAKE ME FEEL?

-
-
-
-

CHALLENGES

-
-
-
-

HOW CAN I IMPROVE IT?

-
-
-
-

ACCOMPLISHED GOALS	UNACCOMPLISHED GOALS	GOALS NEXT MONTH

HABITS RETAINED	HABITS ELIMINATED	NEW HABITS DEVELOPED

THREE THINGS THAT I AM MOST GRATEFUL FOR THIS MONTH

1
2
3

TWO LIFE LESSONS I LEARNED THIS MONTH

1
2

ONE WORD THAT BEST DESCRIBES THIS MONTH

WEEKLY PLANNER

WEEK OF

MOTIVATION

MON

TUE

WED

THUR

FRI

SAT

SUN

TO-DO

TOP PRIORITIES

NOTES

DAILY PLANNER

DATE S M T W T F S

TODAY'S GOALS

TODAY APPOINTMENT

Time	Event

SLEEP

MOOD

WATER INTAKE

Total :

EXERCISE

Total Minutes

Total Steps

MEAL TRACKER

Breakfast

Lunch

Dinner

Snack

THINGS TO GET DONE TODAY

REMINDER

MONEY TRACKER

Money In

Money Out

TODAY I'M GRATEFUL FOR

NOTES

DAILY PLANNER

DATE

S M T W T F S

TODAY'S GOALS

TODAY APPOINTMENT

Time	Event

SLEEP

MOOD

WATER INTAKE

Total :

EXERCISE

Total Minutes

Total Steps

MEAL TRACKER

Breakfast

Lunch

Dinner

Snack

THINGS TO GET DONE TODAY

REMINDER

TODAY I'M GRATEFUL FOR

NOTES

MONEY TRACKER

Money In

Money Out

DAILY PLANNER

DATE S M T W T F S

TODAY'S GOALS

TODAY APPOINTMENT

Time	Event

SLEEP

MOOD

WATER INTAKE

Total :

EXERCISE

Total Minutes

Total Steps

MEAL TRACKER

Breakfast

Lunch

Dinner

Snack

THINGS TO GET DONE TODAY

REMINDER

TODAY I'M GRATEFUL FOR

NOTES

MONEY TRACKER

Money In	Money Out

DAILY PLANNER

DATE

S M T W T F S

TODAY'S GOALS

TODAY APPOINTMENT

Time	Event

SLEEP

MOOD

WATER INTAKE

Total :

EXERCISE

Total Minutes

Total Steps

MEAL TRACKER

Breakfast

Lunch

Dinner

Snack

THINGS TO GET DONE TODAY

REMINDER

MONEY TRACKER

Money In

Money Out

TODAY I'M GRATEFUL FOR

NOTES

DAILY PLANNER

DATE S M T W T F S

TODAY'S GOALS

TODAY APPOINTMENT

Time	Event

SLEEP

MOOD

WATER INTAKE

Total :

EXERCISE

Total Minutes

Total Steps

MEAL TRACKER

Breakfast

Lunch

Dinner

Snack

THINGS TO GET DONE TODAY

REMINDER

MONEY TRACKER

Money In	Money Out

TODAY I'M GRATEFUL FOR

NOTES

DAILY PLANNER

DATE

S M T W T F S

TODAY'S GOALS

TODAY APPOINTMENT

Time	Event

SLEEP

MOOD

WATER INTAKE

Total :

EXERCISE

Total Minutes

Total Steps

MEAL TRACKER

Breakfast

Lunch

Dinner

Snack

THINGS TO GET DONE TODAY

REMINDER

TODAY I'M GRATEFUL FOR

NOTES

MONEY TRACKER

Money In	Money Out

DAILY PLANNER

DATE S M T W T F S

TODAY'S GOALS

TODAY APPOINTMENT

Time	Event

SLEEP

MOOD

WATER INTAKE

Total :

EXERCISE

Total Minutes

Total Steps

THINGS TO GET DONE TODAY

MEAL TRACKER

Breakfast

Lunch

Dinner

Snack

REMINDER

MONEY TRACKER

Money In	Money Out

TODAY I'M GRATEFUL FOR

NOTES

WEEKLY PLANNER

WEEK OF

MOTIVATION

MON

TUE

WED

THUR

FRI

SAT

SUN

TO-DO

TOP PRIORITIES

NOTES

DAILY PLANNER

DATE S M T W T F S

TODAY'S GOALS

TODAY APPOINTMENT

Time	Event

SLEEP

MOOD

WATER INTAKE

Total :

EXERCISE

Total Minutes

Total Steps

THINGS TO GET DONE TODAY

MEAL TRACKER

Breakfast

Lunch

Dinner

Snack

REMINDER

TODAY I'M GRATEFUL FOR

NOTES

MONEY TRACKER

Money In	Money Out

DAILY PLANNER

DATE

S M T W T F S

TODAY'S GOALS

TODAY APPOINTMENT

Time	Event

SLEEP

MOOD

WATER INTAKE

Total :

EXERCISE

Total Minutes

Total Steps

THINGS TO GET DONE TODAY

MEAL TRACKER

Breakfast

Lunch

Dinner

Snack

REMINDER

TODAY I'M GRATEFUL FOR

NOTES

MONEY TRACKER

Money In	Money Out

DAILY PLANNER

DATE S M T W T F S

TODAY'S GOALS

TODAY APPOINTMENT

Time	Event

SLEEP

MOOD

WATER INTAKE

Total :

EXERCISE

Total Minutes

Total Steps

MEAL TRACKER

Breakfast

Lunch

Dinner

Snack

THINGS TO GET DONE TODAY

REMINDER

MONEY TRACKER

Money In

Money Out

TODAY I'M GRATEFUL FOR

NOTES

DAILY PLANNER

DATE

S M T W T F S

TODAY'S GOALS

TODAY APPOINTMENT

Time	Event

SLEEP

MOOD

WATER INTAKE

Total :

EXERCISE

Total Minutes

Total Steps

THINGS TO GET DONE TODAY

MEAL TRACKER

Breakfast

Lunch

Dinner

Snack

REMINDER

MONEY TRACKER

Money In	Money Out

TODAY I'M GRATEFUL FOR

NOTES

DAILY PLANNER

DATE S M T W T F S

TODAY'S GOALS

TODAY APPOINTMENT

Time	Event

SLEEP

MOOD

WATER INTAKE

Total :

EXERCISE

Total Minutes

Total Steps

MEAL TRACKER

Breakfast

Lunch

Dinner

Snack

THINGS TO GET DONE TODAY

REMINDER

MONEY TRACKER

Money In	Money Out

TODAY I'M GRATEFUL FOR

NOTES

DAILY PLANNER

DATE

S M T W T F S

TODAY'S GOALS

TODAY APPOINTMENT

Time	Event

SLEEP

MOOD

WATER INTAKE

Total :

EXERCISE

Total Minutes

Total Steps

MEAL TRACKER

Breakfast

Lunch

Dinner

Snack

THINGS TO GET DONE TODAY

REMINDER

MONEY TRACKER

Money In

Money Out

TODAY I'M GRATEFUL FOR

NOTES

DAILY PLANNER

DATE S M T W T F S

TODAY'S GOALS

TODAY APPOINTMENT

Time	Event

SLEEP

MOOD

WATER INTAKE

Total :

EXERCISE

Total Minutes

Total Steps

THINGS TO GET DONE TODAY

MEAL TRACKER

Breakfast

Lunch

Dinner

Snack

REMINDER

TODAY I'M GRATEFUL FOR

NOTES

MONEY TRACKER

Money In	Money Out

WEEKLY PLANNER

WEEK OF

MOTIVATION

MON

TUE

WED

THUR

FRI

SAT

SUN

TO-DO

TOP PRIORITIES

NOTES

DAILY PLANNER

DATE S M T W T F S

TODAY'S GOALS

TODAY APPOINTMENT

Time	Event

SLEEP

MOOD

WATER INTAKE

Total :

EXERCISE

Total Minutes

Total Steps

MEAL TRACKER

Breakfast

Lunch

Dinner

Snack

THINGS TO GET DONE TODAY

REMINDER

TODAY I'M GRATEFUL FOR

NOTES

MONEY TRACKER

Money In	Money Out

DAILY PLANNER

DATE

S M T W T F S

TODAY'S GOALS

TODAY APPOINTMENT

Time	Event

SLEEP

MOOD

WATER INTAKE

Total :

EXERCISE

Total Minutes

Total Steps

THINGS TO GET DONE TODAY

MEAL TRACKER

Breakfast

Lunch

Dinner

Snack

REMINDER

MONEY TRACKER

Money In	Money Out

TODAY I'M GRATEFUL FOR

NOTES

DAILY PLANNER

DATE S M T W T F S

TODAY'S GOALS

TODAY APPOINTMENT

Time	Event

SLEEP

MOOD

WATER INTAKE

Total :

EXERCISE

Total Minutes

Total Steps

THINGS TO GET DONE TODAY

MEAL TRACKER

Breakfast

Lunch

Dinner

Snack

REMINDER

TODAY I'M GRATEFUL FOR

NOTES

MONEY TRACKER

Money In	Money Out

DAILY PLANNER

DATE

S M T W T F S

TODAY'S GOALS

TODAY APPOINTMENT

Time	Event

SLEEP

MOOD

WATER INTAKE

Total :

EXERCISE

Total Minutes

Total Steps

MEAL TRACKER

Breakfast

Lunch

Dinner

Snack

THINGS TO GET DONE TODAY

REMINDER

MONEY TRACKER

Money In

Money Out

TODAY I'M GRATEFUL FOR

NOTES

DAILY PLANNER

DATE S M T W T F S

TODAY'S GOALS

TODAY APPOINTMENT

Time	Event

SLEEP

MOOD

WATER INTAKE

Total :

EXERCISE

Total Minutes

Total Steps

MEAL TRACKER

Breakfast

Lunch

Dinner

Snack

THINGS TO GET DONE TODAY

REMINDER

MONEY TRACKER

Money In	Money Out

TODAY I'M GRATEFUL FOR

NOTES

DAILY PLANNER

DATE

S M T W T F S

TODAY'S GOALS

TODAY APPOINTMENT

Time	Event

SLEEP

MOOD

WATER INTAKE

Total :

EXERCISE

Total Minutes

Total Steps

THINGS TO GET DONE TODAY

MEAL TRACKER

Breakfast

Lunch

Dinner

Snack

REMINDER

TODAY I'M GRATEFUL FOR

NOTES

MONEY TRACKER

Money In	Money Out

DAILY PLANNER

DATE S M T W T F S

TODAY'S GOALS

TODAY APPOINTMENT

Time	Event

SLEEP

MOOD

WATER INTAKE

Total :

EXERCISE

Total Minutes

Total Steps

THINGS TO GET DONE TODAY

MEAL TRACKER

Breakfast

Lunch

Dinner

Snack

REMINDER

MONEY TRACKER

Money In	Money Out

TODAY I'M GRATEFUL FOR

NOTES

WEEKLY PLANNER

WEEK OF

MOTIVATION

MON

TUE

WED

THUR

FRI

SAT

SUN

TO-DO

TOP PRIORITIES

NOTES

DAILY PLANNER

DATE S M T W T F S

TODAY'S GOALS

TODAY APPOINTMENT

Time	Event

SLEEP

MOOD

WATER INTAKE

Total :

EXERCISE

Total Minutes

Total Steps

MEAL TRACKER

Breakfast

Lunch

Dinner

Snack

THINGS TO GET DONE TODAY

REMINDER

TODAY I'M GRATEFUL FOR

NOTES

MONEY TRACKER

Money In	Money Out

DAILY PLANNER

DATE

S M T W T F S

TODAY'S GOALS

TODAY APPOINTMENT

Time	Event

SLEEP

MOOD

WATER INTAKE

Total :

EXERCISE

Total Minutes

Total Steps

THINGS TO GET DONE TODAY

MEAL TRACKER

Breakfast

Lunch

Dinner

Snack

REMINDER

TODAY I'M GRATEFUL FOR

NOTES

MONEY TRACKER

Money In	Money Out

DAILY PLANNER

DATE S M T W T F S

TODAY'S GOALS

TODAY APPOINTMENT

Time	Event

SLEEP

MOOD

WATER INTAKE

Total :

EXERCISE

Total Minutes

Total Steps

THINGS TO GET DONE TODAY

MEAL TRACKER

Breakfast

Lunch

Dinner

Snack

REMINDER

TODAY I'M GRATEFUL FOR

NOTES

MONEY TRACKER

Money In	Money Out

DAILY PLANNER

DATE

S M T W T F S

TODAY'S GOALS

TODAY APPOINTMENT

Time	Event

SLEEP

MOOD

WATER INTAKE

Total :

EXERCISE

Total Minutes

Total Steps

THINGS TO GET DONE TODAY

MEAL TRACKER

Breakfast

Lunch

Dinner

Snack

REMINDER

TODAY I'M GRATEFUL FOR

NOTES

MONEY TRACKER

Money In	Money Out

DAILY PLANNER

DATE

S M T W T F S

TODAY'S GOALS

TODAY APPOINTMENT

Time	Event

SLEEP

MOOD

WATER INTAKE

Total :

EXERCISE

Total Minutes

Total Steps

MEAL TRACKER

Breakfast

Lunch

Dinner

Snack

THINGS TO GET DONE TODAY

REMINDER

TODAY I'M GRATEFUL FOR

NOTES

MONEY TRACKER

Money In	Money Out

DAILY PLANNER

DATE

S M T W T F S

TODAY'S GOALS

TODAY APPOINTMENT

Time	Event

SLEEP

MOOD

WATER INTAKE

Total :

EXERCISE

Total Minutes

Total Steps

MEAL TRACKER

Breakfast

Lunch

Dinner

Snack

THINGS TO GET DONE TODAY

REMINDER

MONEY TRACKER

Money In	Money Out

TODAY I'M GRATEFUL FOR

NOTES

DAILY PLANNER

DATE S M T W T F S

TODAY'S GOALS

TODAY APPOINTMENT

Time	Event

SLEEP

MOOD

WATER INTAKE

Total :

EXERCISE

Total Minutes

Total Steps

MEAL TRACKER

Breakfast

Lunch

Dinner

Snack

THINGS TO GET DONE TODAY

REMINDER

MONEY TRACKER

Money In	Money Out

TODAY I'M GRATEFUL FOR

NOTES

DAILY PLANNER

DATE

S M T W T F S

TODAY'S GOALS

TODAY APPOINTMENT

Time	Event

SLEEP

MOOD

WATER INTAKE

Total :

EXERCISE

Total Minutes

Total Steps

MEAL TRACKER

Breakfast

Lunch

Dinner

Snack

THINGS TO GET DONE TODAY

REMINDER

TODAY I'M GRATEFUL FOR

NOTES

MONEY TRACKER

Money In	Money Out

DAILY PLANNER

DATE S M T W T F S

TODAY'S GOALS

TODAY APPOINTMENT

Time	Event

SLEEP

MOOD

WATER INTAKE

Total :

EXERCISE

Total Minutes

Total Steps

MEAL TRACKER

Breakfast

Lunch

Dinner

Snack

THINGS TO GET DONE TODAY

REMINDER

MONEY TRACKER

Money In	Money Out

TODAY I'M GRATEFUL FOR

NOTES

DAILY PLANNER

DATE

S M T W T F S

TODAY'S GOALS

TODAY APPOINTMENT

Time	Event

SLEEP

MOOD

WATER INTAKE

Total :

EXERCISE

Total Minutes

Total Steps

THINGS TO GET DONE TODAY

MEAL TRACKER

Breakfast

Lunch

Dinner

Snack

REMINDER

TODAY I'M GRATEFUL FOR

NOTES

MONEY TRACKER

Money In	Money Out

NOTES

JUNE

Monday	Tuesday	Wednesday	Thursday

To-Do

Affirmations For The month

Important Dates

Habits

To start	To stop

What do I love about myself?

Friday	Saturday	Sunday

Self-Care Activities

Main Goals

Appointments

Notes

JUNE BUDGET

Source Of Income	Amount
	$
	$
	$
Total Income	$

Expenses

Date	Bills	Budget	Actual
		$	$
		$	$
		$	$
		$	$
		$	$
		$	$
		$	$
		$	$
		$	$
		$	$
Total		$	$

Date	Groceries	Budget	Actual
		$	$
		$	$
		$	$
		$	$
		$	$
		$	$
		$	$
Total		$	$

Date	Transportation	Budget	Actual
		$	$
		$	$
		$	$
Total		$	$

Date	Shopping	Budget	Actual
		$	$
		$	$
		$	$
		$	$
		$	$
		$	$
Total		$	$

Date	Entertainment	Budget	Actual
		$	$
		$	$
		$	$
Total		$	$

Date	Fees & Charges	Budget	Actual
		$	$
		$	$
		$	$
Total		$	$

Date	Saving	Goal	Needed
		$	$
		$	$
		$	$
Total		$	$

TIME TRACKER

Use a green marker to highlight the hours you are focused and working on your goals. Over the course of the month – revisit and see what your productivity looks like.

DATE	AM												PM											
1	1	2	3	4	5	6	7	8	9	10	11	12	1	2	3	4	5	6	7	8	9	10	11	12
2	1	2	3	4	5	6	7	8	9	10	11	12	1	2	3	4	5	6	7	8	9	10	11	12
3	1	2	3	4	5	6	7	8	9	10	11	12	1	2	3	4	5	6	7	8	9	10	11	12
4	1	2	3	4	5	6	7	8	9	10	11	12	1	2	3	4	5	6	7	8	9	10	11	12
5	1	2	3	4	5	6	7	8	9	10	11	12	1	2	3	4	5	6	7	8	9	10	11	12
6	1	2	3	4	5	6	7	8	9	10	11	12	1	2	3	4	5	6	7	8	9	10	11	12
7	1	2	3	4	5	6	7	8	9	10	11	12	1	2	3	4	5	6	7	8	9	10	11	12
8	1	2	3	4	5	6	7	8	9	10	11	12	1	2	3	4	5	6	7	8	9	10	11	12
9	1	2	3	4	5	6	7	8	9	10	11	12	1	2	3	4	5	6	7	8	9	10	11	12
10	1	2	3	4	5	6	7	8	9	10	11	12	1	2	3	4	5	6	7	8	9	10	11	12
11	1	2	3	4	5	6	7	8	9	10	11	12	1	2	3	4	5	6	7	8	9	10	11	12
12	1	2	3	4	5	6	7	8	9	10	11	12	1	2	3	4	5	6	7	8	9	10	11	12
13	1	2	3	4	5	6	7	8	9	10	11	12	1	2	3	4	5	6	7	8	9	10	11	12
14	1	2	3	4	5	6	7	8	9	10	11	12	1	2	3	4	5	6	7	8	9	10	11	12
15	1	2	3	4	5	6	7	8	9	10	11	12	1	2	3	4	5	6	7	8	9	10	11	12
16	1	2	3	4	5	6	7	8	9	10	11	12	1	2	3	4	5	6	7	8	9	10	11	12
17	1	2	3	4	5	6	7	8	9	10	11	12	1	2	3	4	5	6	7	8	9	10	11	12
18	1	2	3	4	5	6	7	8	9	10	11	12	1	2	3	4	5	6	7	8	9	10	11	12
19	1	2	3	4	5	6	7	8	9	10	11	12	1	2	3	4	5	6	7	8	9	10	11	12
20	1	2	3	4	5	6	7	8	9	10	11	12	1	2	3	4	5	6	7	8	9	10	11	12
21	1	2	3	4	5	6	7	8	9	10	11	12	1	2	3	4	5	6	7	8	9	10	11	12
22	1	2	3	4	5	6	7	8	9	10	11	12	1	2	3	4	5	6	7	8	9	10	11	12
23	1	2	3	4	5	6	7	8	9	10	11	12	1	2	3	4	5	6	7	8	9	10	11	12
24	1	2	3	4	5	6	7	8	9	10	11	12	1	2	3	4	5	6	7	8	9	10	11	12
25	1	2	3	4	5	6	7	8	9	10	11	12	1	2	3	4	5	6	7	8	9	10	11	12
26	1	2	3	4	5	6	7	8	9	10	11	12	1	2	3	4	5	6	7	8	9	10	11	12
27	1	2	3	4	5	6	7	8	9	10	11	12	1	2	3	4	5	6	7	8	9	10	11	12
28	1	2	3	4	5	6	7	8	9	10	11	12	1	2	3	4	5	6	7	8	9	10	11	12
29	1	2	3	4	5	6	7	8	9	10	11	12	1	2	3	4	5	6	7	8	9	10	11	12
30	1	2	3	4	5	6	7	8	9	10	11	12	1	2	3	4	5	6	7	8	9	10	11	12
31	1	2	3	4	5	6	7	8	9	10	11	12	1	2	3	4	5	6	7	8	9	10	11	12

CLIENT INFORMATION

Name
Phone
Email
Website
Address
Billing Adress
City
State Zip
D.O.B
Business Hours

Additional Information

Name
Phone
Email
Website
Address
Billing Adress
City
State Zip
D.O.B
Business Hours

Additional Information

Name
Phone
Email
Website
Address
Billing Adress
City
State Zip
D.O.B
Business Hours

Additional Information

Name
Phone
Email
Website
Address
Billing Adress
City
State Zip
D.O.B
Business Hours

Additional Information

CLIENT INFORMATION

Name
Phone
Email
Website
Address
Billing Adress
City
State Zip
D.O.B
Business Hours

Additional Information

Name
Phone
Email
Website
Address
Billing Adress
City
State Zip
D.O.B
Business Hours

Additional Information

Name
Phone
Email
Website
Address
Billing Adress
City
State Zip
D.O.B
Business Hours

Additional Information

Name
Phone
Email
Website
Address
Billing Adress
City
State Zip
D.O.B
Business Hours

Additional Information

MEETING NOTES

SUBJECT	DATE	TIME

AGENDA

ATTENDEES

IMPORTANT NOTES

SUBJECT	DATE	TIME

AGENDA

ATTENDEES

IMPORTANT NOTES

MEETING NOTES

SUBJECT	DATE	TIME

AGENDA

ATTENDEES	IMPORTANT NOTES

SUBJECT	DATE	TIME

AGENDA

ATTENDEES	IMPORTANT NOTES

JUNE SELF-CARE

Write a self-care activity and tick off each time you do self-care act.

ACTIVITIES	CHECKLIST
	1 2 3 4 5 6 7 8 9 10 11 12 13 14 15 16 17 18 19 20 21 22 23 24 25 26 27 28 29 30 31
	1 2 3 4 5 6 7 8 9 10 11 12 13 14 15 16 17 18 19 20 21 22 23 24 25 26 27 28 29 30 31
	1 2 3 4 5 6 7 8 9 10 11 12 13 14 15 16 17 18 19 20 21 22 23 24 25 26 27 28 29 30 31
	1 2 3 4 5 6 7 8 9 10 11 12 13 14 15 16 17 18 19 20 21 22 23 24 25 26 27 28 29 30 31
	1 2 3 4 5 6 7 8 9 10 11 12 13 14 15 16 17 18 19 20 21 22 23 24 25 26 27 28 29 30 31
	1 2 3 4 5 6 7 8 9 10 11 12 13 14 15 16 17 18 19 20 21 22 23 24 25 26 27 28 29 30 31
	1 2 3 4 5 6 7 8 9 10 11 12 13 14 15 16 17 18 19 20 21 22 23 24 25 26 27 28 29 30 31
	1 2 3 4 5 6 7 8 9 10 11 12 13 14 15 16 17 18 19 20 21 22 23 24 25 26 27 28 29 30 31
	1 2 3 4 5 6 7 8 9 10 11 12 13 14 15 16 17 18 19 20 21 22 23 24 25 26 27 28 29 30 31
	1 2 3 4 5 6 7 8 9 10 11 12 13 14 15 16 17 18 19 20 21 22 23 24 25 26 27 28 29 30 31

REFLECTION

HOW WILL YOU RATE THIS MONTH? ☆ ☆ ☆ ☆ ☆ ☆ ☆ ☆ ☆ ☆

MONTHLY WINS

-
-
-
-

HOW DOES IT MAKE ME FEEL?

-
-
-
-

CHALLENGES

-
-
-
-

HOW CAN I IMPROVE IT?

-
-
-
-

ACCOMPLISHED GOALS

UNACCOMPLISHED GOALS

GOALS NEXT MONTH

HABITS RETAINED

HABITS ELIMINATED

NEW HABITS DEVELOPED

THREE THINGS THAT I AM MOST GRATEFUL FOR THIS MONTH

1

2

3

TWO LIFE LESSONS I LEARNED THIS MONTH

1

2

ONE WORD THAT BEST DESCRIBES THIS MONTH

WEEKLY PLANNER

WEEK OF

MOTIVATION

MON

TUE

WED

THUR

FRI

SAT

SUN

TO-DO

TOP PRIORITIES

NOTES

DAILY PLANNER

DATE S M T W T F S

TODAY'S GOALS

TODAY APPOINTMENT

Time	Event

SLEEP

MOOD

WATER INTAKE

Total :

EXERCISE

Total Minutes

Total Steps

THINGS TO GET DONE TODAY

MEAL TRACKER

Breakfast

Lunch

Dinner

Snack

REMINDER

TODAY I'M GRATEFUL FOR

NOTES

MONEY TRACKER

Money In	Money Out

DAILY PLANNER

DATE

S M T W T F S

TODAY'S GOALS

TODAY APPOINTMENT

Time	Event

SLEEP

MOOD

WATER INTAKE

Total :

EXERCISE

Total Minutes

Total Steps

THINGS TO GET DONE TODAY

MEAL TRACKER

Breakfast

Lunch

Dinner

Snack

REMINDER

TODAY I'M GRATEFUL FOR

NOTES

MONEY TRACKER

Money In	Money Out

DAILY PLANNER

DATE S M T W T F S

TODAY'S GOALS

TODAY APPOINTMENT

Time	Event

SLEEP

MOOD

WATER INTAKE

Total :

EXERCISE

Total Minutes

Total Steps

MEAL TRACKER

Breakfast

Lunch

Dinner

Snack

THINGS TO GET DONE TODAY

REMINDER

MONEY TRACKER

Money In

Money Out

TODAY I'M GRATEFUL FOR

NOTES

DAILY PLANNER

DATE

S M T W T F S

TODAY'S GOALS

TODAY APPOINTMENT

Time	Event

SLEEP

MOOD

WATER INTAKE

Total :

EXERCISE

Total Minutes

Total Steps

THINGS TO GET DONE TODAY

MEAL TRACKER

Breakfast

Lunch

Dinner

Snack

REMINDER

TODAY I'M GRATEFUL FOR

NOTES

MONEY TRACKER

Money In	Money Out

DAILY PLANNER

DATE S M T W T F S

TODAY'S GOALS

TODAY APPOINTMENT

Time	Event

SLEEP

MOOD

WATER INTAKE

Total :

EXERCISE

Total Minutes

Total Steps

MEAL TRACKER

Breakfast

Lunch

Dinner

Snack

THINGS TO GET DONE TODAY

REMINDER

TODAY I'M GRATEFUL FOR

NOTES

MONEY TRACKER

Money In	Money Out

DAILY PLANNER

DATE

S M T W T F S

TODAY'S GOALS

TODAY APPOINTMENT

Time	Event

SLEEP

MOOD

WATER INTAKE

Total :

EXERCISE

Total Minutes

Total Steps

MEAL TRACKER

Breakfast

Lunch

Dinner

Snack

THINGS TO GET DONE TODAY

REMINDER

TODAY I'M GRATEFUL FOR

NOTES

MONEY TRACKER

Money In	Money Out

DAILY PLANNER

DATE S M T W T F S

TODAY'S GOALS

TODAY APPOINTMENT

Time	Event

SLEEP

MOOD

WATER INTAKE

Total :

EXERCISE

Total Minutes

Total Steps

MEAL TRACKER

Breakfast

Lunch

Dinner

Snack

THINGS TO GET DONE TODAY

REMINDER

MONEY TRACKER

Money In

Money Out

TODAY I'M GRATEFUL FOR

NOTES

WEEKLY PLANNER

WEEK OF

MOTIVATION

MON

TUE

WED

THUR

FRI

SAT

SUN

TO-DO

TOP PRIORITIES

NOTES

DAILY PLANNER

DATE S M T W T F S

TODAY'S GOALS

TODAY APPOINTMENT

Time	Event

SLEEP

MOOD

WATER INTAKE

Total :

EXERCISE

Total Minutes

Total Steps

THINGS TO GET DONE TODAY

MEAL TRACKER

Breakfast

Lunch

Dinner

Snack

REMINDER

TODAY I'M GRATEFUL FOR

NOTES

MONEY TRACKER

Money In	Money Out

DAILY PLANNER

DATE

S M T W T F S

TODAY'S GOALS

TODAY APPOINTMENT

Time	Event

SLEEP

MOOD

WATER INTAKE

Total :

EXERCISE

Total Minutes

Total Steps

THINGS TO GET DONE TODAY

MEAL TRACKER

Breakfast

Lunch

Dinner

Snack

REMINDER

TODAY I'M GRATEFUL FOR

NOTES

MONEY TRACKER

Money In	Money Out

DAILY PLANNER

DATE S M T W T F S

TODAY'S GOALS

TODAY APPOINTMENT

Time	Event

SLEEP

MOOD

WATER INTAKE

Total :

THINGS TO GET DONE TODAY

EXERCISE

Total Minutes

Total Steps

MEAL TRACKER

Breakfast

Lunch

Dinner

Snack

REMINDER

TODAY I'M GRATEFUL FOR

NOTES

MONEY TRACKER

Money In	Money Out

DAILY PLANNER

DATE

S M T W T F S

TODAY'S GOALS

TODAY APPOINTMENT

Time	Event

SLEEP

MOOD

WATER INTAKE

Total :

EXERCISE

Total Minutes

Total Steps

THINGS TO GET DONE TODAY

MEAL TRACKER

Breakfast

Lunch

Dinner

Snack

REMINDER

TODAY I'M GRATEFUL FOR

NOTES

MONEY TRACKER

Money In	Money Out

DAILY PLANNER

DATE S M T W T F S

TODAY'S GOALS

TODAY APPOINTMENT

Time	Event

SLEEP

MOOD

WATER INTAKE

Total :

EXERCISE

Total Minutes

Total Steps

MEAL TRACKER

Breakfast

Lunch

Dinner

Snack

THINGS TO GET DONE TODAY

REMINDER

MONEY TRACKER

Money In	Money Out

TODAY I'M GRATEFUL FOR

NOTES

DAILY PLANNER

DATE

S M T W T F S

TODAY'S GOALS

TODAY APPOINTMENT

Time	Event

SLEEP

MOOD

WATER INTAKE

Total :

EXERCISE

Total Minutes

Total Steps

THINGS TO GET DONE TODAY

MEAL TRACKER

Breakfast

Lunch

Dinner

Snack

REMINDER

TODAY I'M GRATEFUL FOR

NOTES

MONEY TRACKER

Money In	Money Out

DAILY PLANNER

DATE S M T W T F S

TODAY'S GOALS

TODAY APPOINTMENT

Time	Event

SLEEP

MOOD

WATER INTAKE

Total :

EXERCISE

Total Minutes

Total Steps

THINGS TO GET DONE TODAY

MEAL TRACKER

Breakfast

Lunch

Dinner

Snack

REMINDER

TODAY I'M GRATEFUL FOR

NOTES

MONEY TRACKER

Money In	Money Out

WEEKLY PLANNER

WEEK OF

MOTIVATION

MON

TUE

WED

THUR

FRI

SAT

SUN

TO-DO

TOP PRIORITIES

NOTES

DAILY PLANNER

DATE S M T W T F S

TODAY'S GOALS

TODAY APPOINTMENT

Time	Event

SLEEP

MOOD

WATER INTAKE

Total :

EXERCISE

Total Minutes

Total Steps

THINGS TO GET DONE TODAY

MEAL TRACKER

Breakfast

Lunch

Dinner

Snack

REMINDER

TODAY I'M GRATEFUL FOR

NOTES

MONEY TRACKER

Money In	Money Out

DAILY PLANNER

DATE

S M T W T F S

TODAY'S GOALS

TODAY APPOINTMENT

Time	Event

SLEEP

MOOD

WATER INTAKE

Total :

EXERCISE

Total Minutes

Total Steps

MEAL TRACKER

Breakfast

Lunch

Dinner

Snack

THINGS TO GET DONE TODAY

REMINDER

TODAY I'M GRATEFUL FOR

NOTES

MONEY TRACKER

Money In

Money Out

DAILY PLANNER

DATE S M T W T F S

TODAY'S GOALS

TODAY APPOINTMENT

Time	Event

SLEEP

MOOD

WATER INTAKE

Total :

THINGS TO GET DONE TODAY

EXERCISE

Total Minutes

Total Steps

MEAL TRACKER

Breakfast

Lunch

Dinner

Snack

REMINDER

TODAY I'M GRATEFUL FOR

NOTES

MONEY TRACKER

Money In	Money Out

DAILY PLANNER

DATE

S M T W T F S

TODAY'S GOALS

TODAY APPOINTMENT

Time	Event

SLEEP

MOOD

WATER INTAKE

Total :

EXERCISE

Total Minutes

Total Steps

MEAL TRACKER

Breakfast

Lunch

Dinner

Snack

THINGS TO GET DONE TODAY

REMINDER

MONEY TRACKER

Money In

Money Out

TODAY I'M GRATEFUL FOR

NOTES

DAILY PLANNER

DATE S M T W T F S

TODAY'S GOALS

TODAY APPOINTMENT

Time	Event

SLEEP

MOOD

WATER INTAKE

Total :

EXERCISE

Total Minutes

Total Steps

MEAL TRACKER

Breakfast

Lunch

Dinner

Snack

THINGS TO GET DONE TODAY

REMINDER

TODAY I'M GRATEFUL FOR

NOTES

MONEY TRACKER

Money In	Money Out

DAILY PLANNER

DATE

S M T W T F S

TODAY'S GOALS

TODAY APPOINTMENT

Time	Event

SLEEP

MOOD

WATER INTAKE

Total :

EXERCISE

Total Minutes

Total Steps

MEAL TRACKER

Breakfast

Lunch

Dinner

Snack

THINGS TO GET DONE TODAY

REMINDER

MONEY TRACKER

Money In	Money Out

TODAY I'M GRATEFUL FOR

NOTES

DAILY PLANNER

DATE S M T W T F S

TODAY'S GOALS

TODAY APPOINTMENT

Time	Event

SLEEP

MOOD

WATER INTAKE

Total :

EXERCISE

Total Minutes

Total Steps

MEAL TRACKER

Breakfast

Lunch

Dinner

Snack

THINGS TO GET DONE TODAY

REMINDER

TODAY I'M GRATEFUL FOR

NOTES

MONEY TRACKER

Money In	Money Out

WEEKLY PLANNER

WEEK OF	
MOTIVATION	

MON

TUE

WED

THUR

FRI

SAT

SUN

TO-DO

TOP PRIORITIES

NOTES

DAILY PLANNER

DATE S M T W T F S

TODAY'S GOALS

TODAY APPOINTMENT

Time	Event

SLEEP

MOOD

WATER INTAKE

Total :

EXERCISE

Total Minutes

Total Steps

THINGS TO GET DONE TODAY

MEAL TRACKER

Breakfast

Lunch

Dinner

Snack

REMINDER

TODAY I'M GRATEFUL FOR

NOTES

MONEY TRACKER

Money In	Money Out

DAILY PLANNER

DATE

S M T W T F S

TODAY'S GOALS

TODAY APPOINTMENT

Time	Event

SLEEP

MOOD

WATER INTAKE

Total :

EXERCISE

Total Minutes

Total Steps

MEAL TRACKER

Breakfast

Lunch

Dinner

Snack

THINGS TO GET DONE TODAY

REMINDER

TODAY I'M GRATEFUL FOR

NOTES

MONEY TRACKER

Money In	Money Out

DAILY PLANNER

DATE S M T W T F S

TODAY'S GOALS

TODAY APPOINTMENT

Time	Event

SLEEP

MOOD

WATER INTAKE

Total :

EXERCISE

Total Minutes

Total Steps

THINGS TO GET DONE TODAY

MEAL TRACKER

Breakfast

Lunch

Dinner

Snack

REMINDER

MONEY TRACKER

Money In	Money Out

TODAY I'M GRATEFUL FOR

NOTES

DAILY PLANNER

DATE

S M T W T F S

TODAY'S GOALS

TODAY APPOINTMENT

Time	Event

SLEEP

MOOD

WATER INTAKE

Total :

EXERCISE

Total Minutes

Total Steps

MEAL TRACKER

Breakfast

Lunch

Dinner

Snack

THINGS TO GET DONE TODAY

REMINDER

MONEY TRACKER

Money In	Money Out

TODAY I'M GRATEFUL FOR

NOTES

DAILY PLANNER

DATE S M T W T F S

TODAY'S GOALS

TODAY APPOINTMENT

Time	Event

SLEEP

MOOD

WATER INTAKE

Total :

EXERCISE

Total Minutes

Total Steps

THINGS TO GET DONE TODAY

MEAL TRACKER

Breakfast

Lunch

Dinner

Snack

REMINDER

TODAY I'M GRATEFUL FOR

NOTES

MONEY TRACKER

Money In	Money Out

DAILY PLANNER

DATE

S M T W T F S

TODAY'S GOALS

TODAY APPOINTMENT

Time	Event

SLEEP

MOOD

WATER INTAKE

Total :

EXERCISE

Total Minutes

Total Steps

MEAL TRACKER

Breakfast

Lunch

Dinner

Snack

THINGS TO GET DONE TODAY

REMINDER

MONEY TRACKER

Money In	Money Out

TODAY I'M GRATEFUL FOR

NOTES

DAILY PLANNER

DATE S M T W T F S

TODAY'S GOALS

TODAY APPOINTMENT

Time	Event

SLEEP

MOOD

WATER INTAKE

Total :

EXERCISE

Total Minutes

Total Steps

MEAL TRACKER

Breakfast

Lunch

Dinner

Snack

THINGS TO GET DONE TODAY

REMINDER

TODAY I'M GRATEFUL FOR

NOTES

MONEY TRACKER

Money In	Money Out

DAILY PLANNER

DATE

S M T W T F S

TODAY'S GOALS

TODAY APPOINTMENT

Time	Event

SLEEP

MOOD

WATER INTAKE

Total :

EXERCISE

Total Minutes

Total Steps

THINGS TO GET DONE TODAY

MEAL TRACKER

Breakfast

Lunch

Dinner

Snack

REMINDER

TODAY I'M GRATEFUL FOR

NOTES

MONEY TRACKER

Money In	Money Out

DAILY PLANNER

DATE S M T W T F S

TODAY'S GOALS

TODAY APPOINTMENT

Time	Event

SLEEP

MOOD

WATER INTAKE

Total :

EXERCISE

Total Minutes

Total Steps

MEAL TRACKER

Breakfast

Lunch

Dinner

Snack

THINGS TO GET DONE TODAY

REMINDER

MONEY TRACKER

Money In

Money Out

TODAY I'M GRATEFUL FOR

NOTES

NOTES

NOTES

JULY

To-Do

Affirmations For The month

Monday	Tuesday	Wednesday	Thursday

Important Dates

Habits

To start	To stop

What do I love about myself?

Friday	Saturday	Sunday

Self-Care Activities

Main Goals

Appointments

Notes

JULY BUDGET

Source Of Income	Amount
	$
	$
	$
Total Income	$

Expenses

Date	Bills	Budget	Actual
		$	$
		$	$
		$	$
		$	$
		$	$
		$	$
		$	$
		$	$
		$	$
		$	$
Total		$	$

Date	Groceries	Budget	Actual
		$	$
		$	$
		$	$
		$	$
		$	$
		$	$
		$	$
Total		$	$

Date	Transportation	Budget	Actual
		$	$
		$	$
		$	$
Total		$	$

Date	Shopping	Budget	Actual
		$	$
		$	$
		$	$
		$	$
		$	$
		$	$
Total		$	$

Date	Entertainment	Budget	Actual
		$	$
		$	$
		$	$
Total		$	$

Date	Fees & Charges	Budget	Actual
		$	$
		$	$
		$	$
Total		$	$

Date	Saving	Goal	Needed
		$	$
		$	$
		$	$
Total		$	$

TIME TRACKER

Use a green marker to highlight the hours you are focused and working on your goals. Over the course of the month – revisit and see what your productivity looks like.

DATE	AM												PM											
1	1	2	3	4	5	6	7	8	9	10	11	12	1	2	3	4	5	6	7	8	9	10	11	12
2	1	2	3	4	5	6	7	8	9	10	11	12	1	2	3	4	5	6	7	8	9	10	11	12
3	1	2	3	4	5	6	7	8	9	10	11	12	1	2	3	4	5	6	7	8	9	10	11	12
4	1	2	3	4	5	6	7	8	9	10	11	12	1	2	3	4	5	6	7	8	9	10	11	12
5	1	2	3	4	5	6	7	8	9	10	11	12	1	2	3	4	5	6	7	8	9	10	11	12
6	1	2	3	4	5	6	7	8	9	10	11	12	1	2	3	4	5	6	7	8	9	10	11	12
7	1	2	3	4	5	6	7	8	9	10	11	12	1	2	3	4	5	6	7	8	9	10	11	12
8	1	2	3	4	5	6	7	8	9	10	11	12	1	2	3	4	5	6	7	8	9	10	11	12
9	1	2	3	4	5	6	7	8	9	10	11	12	1	2	3	4	5	6	7	8	9	10	11	12
10	1	2	3	4	5	6	7	8	9	10	11	12	1	2	3	4	5	6	7	8	9	10	11	12
11	1	2	3	4	5	6	7	8	9	10	11	12	1	2	3	4	5	6	7	8	9	10	11	12
12	1	2	3	4	5	6	7	8	9	10	11	12	1	2	3	4	5	6	7	8	9	10	11	12
13	1	2	3	4	5	6	7	8	9	10	11	12	1	2	3	4	5	6	7	8	9	10	11	12
14	1	2	3	4	5	6	7	8	9	10	11	12	1	2	3	4	5	6	7	8	9	10	11	12
15	1	2	3	4	5	6	7	8	9	10	11	12	1	2	3	4	5	6	7	8	9	10	11	12
16	1	2	3	4	5	6	7	8	9	10	11	12	1	2	3	4	5	6	7	8	9	10	11	12
17	1	2	3	4	5	6	7	8	9	10	11	12	1	2	3	4	5	6	7	8	9	10	11	12
18	1	2	3	4	5	6	7	8	9	10	11	12	1	2	3	4	5	6	7	8	9	10	11	12
19	1	2	3	4	5	6	7	8	9	10	11	12	1	2	3	4	5	6	7	8	9	10	11	12
20	1	2	3	4	5	6	7	8	9	10	11	12	1	2	3	4	5	6	7	8	9	10	11	12
21	1	2	3	4	5	6	7	8	9	10	11	12	1	2	3	4	5	6	7	8	9	10	11	12
22	1	2	3	4	5	6	7	8	9	10	11	12	1	2	3	4	5	6	7	8	9	10	11	12
23	1	2	3	4	5	6	7	8	9	10	11	12	1	2	3	4	5	6	7	8	9	10	11	12
24	1	2	3	4	5	6	7	8	9	10	11	12	1	2	3	4	5	6	7	8	9	10	11	12
25	1	2	3	4	5	6	7	8	9	10	11	12	1	2	3	4	5	6	7	8	9	10	11	12
26	1	2	3	4	5	6	7	8	9	10	11	12	1	2	3	4	5	6	7	8	9	10	11	12
27	1	2	3	4	5	6	7	8	9	10	11	12	1	2	3	4	5	6	7	8	9	10	11	12
28	1	2	3	4	5	6	7	8	9	10	11	12	1	2	3	4	5	6	7	8	9	10	11	12
29	1	2	3	4	5	6	7	8	9	10	11	12	1	2	3	4	5	6	7	8	9	10	11	12
30	1	2	3	4	5	6	7	8	9	10	11	12	1	2	3	4	5	6	7	8	9	10	11	12
31	1	2	3	4	5	6	7	8	9	10	11	12	1	2	3	4	5	6	7	8	9	10	11	12

CLIENT INFORMATION

Name
Phone
Email
Website
Address
Billing Adress
City
State Zip
D.O.B
Business Hours

Additional Information

Name
Phone
Email
Website
Address
Billing Adress
City
State Zip
D.O.B
Business Hours

Additional Information

Name
Phone
Email
Website
Address
Billing Adress
City
State Zip
D.O.B
Business Hours

Additional Information

Name
Phone
Email
Website
Address
Billing Adress
City
State Zip
D.O.B
Business Hours

Additional Information

CLIENT INFORMATION

Name
Phone
Email
Website
Address
Billing Adress
City
State Zip
D.O.B
Business Hours

Additional Information

Name
Phone
Email
Website
Address
Billing Adress
City
State Zip
D.O.B
Business Hours

Additional Information

Name
Phone
Email
Website
Address
Billing Adress
City
State Zip
D.O.B
Business Hours

Additional Information

Name
Phone
Email
Website
Address
Billing Adress
City
State Zip
D.O.B
Business Hours

Additional Information

MEETING NOTES

SUBJECT	DATE	TIME

AGENDA

ATTENDEES

-
-
-
-
-

IMPORTANT NOTES

SUBJECT	DATE	TIME

AGENDA

ATTENDEES

-
-
-
-
-

IMPORTANT NOTES

MEETING NOTES

SUBJECT	DATE	TIME

AGENDA

ATTENDEES

IMPORTANT NOTES

SUBJECT	DATE	TIME

AGENDA

ATTENDEES

IMPORTANT NOTES

JULY SELF-CARE

Write a self-care activity and tick off each time you do self-care act.

ACTIVITIES	CHECKLIST
	1 2 3 4 5 6 7 8 9 10 11 12 13 14 15 16 17 18 19 20 21 22 23 24 25 26 27 28 29 30 31
	1 2 3 4 5 6 7 8 9 10 11 12 13 14 15 16 17 18 19 20 21 22 23 24 25 26 27 28 29 30 31
	1 2 3 4 5 6 7 8 9 10 11 12 13 14 15 16 17 18 19 20 21 22 23 24 25 26 27 28 29 30 31
	1 2 3 4 5 6 7 8 9 10 11 12 13 14 15 16 17 18 19 20 21 22 23 24 25 26 27 28 29 30 31
	1 2 3 4 5 6 7 8 9 10 11 12 13 14 15 16 17 18 19 20 21 22 23 24 25 26 27 28 29 30 31
	1 2 3 4 5 6 7 8 9 10 11 12 13 14 15 16 17 18 19 20 21 22 23 24 25 26 27 28 29 30 31
	1 2 3 4 5 6 7 8 9 10 11 12 13 14 15 16 17 18 19 20 21 22 23 24 25 26 27 28 29 30 31
	1 2 3 4 5 6 7 8 9 10 11 12 13 14 15 16 17 18 19 20 21 22 23 24 25 26 27 28 29 30 31
	1 2 3 4 5 6 7 8 9 10 11 12 13 14 15 16 17 18 19 20 21 22 23 24 25 26 27 28 29 30 31
	1 2 3 4 5 6 7 8 9 10 11 12 13 14 15 16 17 18 19 20 21 22 23 24 25 26 27 28 29 30 31

REFLECTION

HOW WILL YOU RATE THIS MONTH? ☆ ☆ ☆ ☆ ☆ ☆ ☆ ☆ ☆ ☆

MONTHLY WINS

-
-
-
-

HOW DOES IT MAKE ME FEEL?

-
-
-
-

CHALLENGES

-
-
-
-

HOW CAN I IMPROVE IT?

-
-
-
-

ACCOMPLISHED GOALS

UNACCOMPLISHED GOALS

GOALS NEXT MONTH

HABITS RETAINED

HABITS ELIMINATED

NEW HABITS DEVELOPED

THREE THINGS THAT I AM MOST GRATEFUL FOR THIS MONTH

1

2

3

TWO LIFE LESSONS I LEARNED THIS MONTH

1

2

ONE WORD THAT BEST DESCRIBES THIS MONTH

WEEKLY PLANNER

WEEK OF

MOTIVATION

MON

TUE

WED

THUR

FRI

SAT

SUN

TO-DO

TOP PRIORITIES

NOTES

DAILY PLANNER

DATE S M T W T F S

TODAY'S GOALS

TODAY APPOINTMENT

Time	Event

SLEEP

MOOD

WATER INTAKE

Total :

EXERCISE

Total Minutes

Total Steps

MEAL TRACKER

Breakfast

Lunch

Dinner

Snack

THINGS TO GET DONE TODAY

REMINDER

TODAY I'M GRATEFUL FOR

NOTES

MONEY TRACKER

Money In	Money Out

DAILY PLANNER

DATE

S M T W T F S

TODAY'S GOALS

TODAY APPOINTMENT

Time	Event

SLEEP

MOOD

WATER INTAKE

Total :

EXERCISE

Total Minutes

Total Steps

THINGS TO GET DONE TODAY

MEAL TRACKER

Breakfast

Lunch

Dinner

Snack

REMINDER

TODAY I'M GRATEFUL FOR

NOTES

MONEY TRACKER

Money In	Money Out

DAILY PLANNER

DATE S M T W T F S

TODAY'S GOALS

TODAY APPOINTMENT

Time	Event

SLEEP

MOOD

WATER INTAKE

Total :

EXERCISE

Total Minutes

Total Steps

MEAL TRACKER

Breakfast

Lunch

Dinner

Snack

THINGS TO GET DONE TODAY

REMINDER

TODAY I'M GRATEFUL FOR

NOTES

MONEY TRACKER

Money In	Money Out

DAILY PLANNER

DATE

S M T W T F S

TODAY'S GOALS

TODAY APPOINTMENT

Time	Event

SLEEP

MOOD

WATER INTAKE

Total :

EXERCISE

Total Minutes

Total Steps

THINGS TO GET DONE TODAY

MEAL TRACKER

Breakfast

Lunch

Dinner

Snack

REMINDER

TODAY I'M GRATEFUL FOR

NOTES

MONEY TRACKER

Money In	Money Out

DAILY PLANNER

DATE S M T W T F S

TODAY'S GOALS

TODAY APPOINTMENT

Time	Event

SLEEP

MOOD

WATER INTAKE

Total :

EXERCISE

Total Minutes

Total Steps

MEAL TRACKER

Breakfast

Lunch

Dinner

Snack

THINGS TO GET DONE TODAY

REMINDER

MONEY TRACKER

Money In	Money Out

TODAY I'M GRATEFUL FOR

NOTES

DAILY PLANNER

DATE

S M T W T F S

TODAY'S GOALS

TODAY APPOINTMENT

Time	Event

SLEEP

MOOD

WATER INTAKE

Total :

EXERCISE

Total Minutes

Total Steps

THINGS TO GET DONE TODAY

MEAL TRACKER

Breakfast

Lunch

Dinner

Snack

REMINDER

TODAY I'M GRATEFUL FOR

NOTES

MONEY TRACKER

Money In	Money Out

DAILY PLANNER

DATE S M T W T F S

TODAY'S GOALS

TODAY APPOINTMENT

Time	Event

SLEEP

MOOD

WATER INTAKE

Total :

EXERCISE

Total Minutes

Total Steps

THINGS TO GET DONE TODAY

MEAL TRACKER

Breakfast

Lunch

Dinner

Snack

REMINDER

TODAY I'M GRATEFUL FOR

NOTES

MONEY TRACKER

Money In	Money Out

WEEKLY PLANNER

WEEK OF

MOTIVATION

MON

TUE

WED

THUR

FRI

SAT

SUN

TO-DO

TOP PRIORITIES

NOTES

DAILY PLANNER

DATE S M T W T F S

TODAY'S GOALS

TODAY APPOINTMENT

Time	Event

SLEEP

MOOD

WATER INTAKE

Total :

EXERCISE

Total Minutes

Total Steps

MEAL TRACKER

Breakfast

Lunch

Dinner

Snack

THINGS TO GET DONE TODAY

REMINDER

MONEY TRACKER

Money In	Money Out

TODAY I'M GRATEFUL FOR

NOTES

DAILY PLANNER

DATE

S M T W T F S

TODAY'S GOALS

TODAY APPOINTMENT

Time	Event

SLEEP

MOOD

WATER INTAKE

Total :

EXERCISE

Total Minutes

Total Steps

THINGS TO GET DONE TODAY

MEAL TRACKER

Breakfast

Lunch

Dinner

Snack

REMINDER

TODAY I'M GRATEFUL FOR

MONEY TRACKER

Money In	Money Out

NOTES

DAILY PLANNER

DATE S M T W T F S

TODAY'S GOALS

TODAY APPOINTMENT

Time	Event

SLEEP

MOOD

WATER INTAKE

Total :

EXERCISE

Total Minutes

Total Steps

THINGS TO GET DONE TODAY

MEAL TRACKER

Breakfast

Lunch

Dinner

Snack

REMINDER

MONEY TRACKER

Money In	Money Out

TODAY I'M GRATEFUL FOR

NOTES

DAILY PLANNER

DATE

S M T W T F S

TODAY'S GOALS

TODAY APPOINTMENT

Time	Event

SLEEP

MOOD

WATER INTAKE

Total :

EXERCISE

Total Minutes

Total Steps

THINGS TO GET DONE TODAY

MEAL TRACKER

Breakfast

Lunch

Dinner

Snack

REMINDER

TODAY I'M GRATEFUL FOR

NOTES

MONEY TRACKER

Money In	Money Out

DAILY PLANNER

DATE S M T W T F S

TODAY'S GOALS

TODAY APPOINTMENT

Time	Event

SLEEP

MOOD

WATER INTAKE

Total :

EXERCISE

Total Minutes

Total Steps

THINGS TO GET DONE TODAY

MEAL TRACKER

Breakfast

Lunch

Dinner

Snack

REMINDER

TODAY I'M GRATEFUL FOR

NOTES

MONEY TRACKER

Money In	Money Out

DAILY PLANNER

DATE

S M T W T F S

TODAY'S GOALS

TODAY APPOINTMENT

Time	Event

SLEEP

MOOD

WATER INTAKE

Total :

EXERCISE

Total Minutes

Total Steps

MEAL TRACKER

Breakfast

Lunch

Dinner

Snack

THINGS TO GET DONE TODAY

REMINDER

TODAY I'M GRATEFUL FOR

NOTES

MONEY TRACKER

Money In	Money Out

DAILY PLANNER

DATE S M T W T F S

TODAY'S GOALS

TODAY APPOINTMENT

Time	Event

SLEEP

MOOD

WATER INTAKE

Total :

EXERCISE

Total Minutes

Total Steps

MEAL TRACKER

Breakfast

Lunch

Dinner

Snack

THINGS TO GET DONE TODAY

REMINDER

MONEY TRACKER

Money In	Money Out

TODAY I'M GRATEFUL FOR

NOTES

WEEKLY PLANNER

WEEK OF

MOTIVATION

MON

TUE

WED

THUR

FRI

SAT

SUN

TO-DO

TOP PRIORITIES

NOTES

DAILY PLANNER

DATE S M T W T F S

TODAY'S GOALS

TODAY APPOINTMENT

Time	Event

SLEEP

MOOD

WATER INTAKE

Total :

EXERCISE

Total Minutes

Total Steps

MEAL TRACKER

Breakfast

Lunch

Dinner

Snack

THINGS TO GET DONE TODAY

REMINDER

MONEY TRACKER

Money In

Money Out

TODAY I'M GRATEFUL FOR

NOTES

DAILY PLANNER

DATE

S M T W T F S

TODAY'S GOALS

TODAY APPOINTMENT

Time	Event

SLEEP

MOOD

WATER INTAKE

Total :

EXERCISE

Total Minutes

Total Steps

MEAL TRACKER

Breakfast

Lunch

Dinner

Snack

THINGS TO GET DONE TODAY

REMINDER

TODAY I'M GRATEFUL FOR

NOTES

MONEY TRACKER

Money In	Money Out

DAILY PLANNER

DATE S M T W T F S

TODAY'S GOALS

TODAY APPOINTMENT

Time	Event

SLEEP

MOOD

WATER INTAKE

Total :

EXERCISE

Total Minutes

Total Steps

MEAL TRACKER

Breakfast

Lunch

Dinner

Snack

THINGS TO GET DONE TODAY

REMINDER

TODAY I'M GRATEFUL FOR

NOTES

MONEY TRACKER

Money In	Money Out

DAILY PLANNER

DATE

S M T W T F S

TODAY'S GOALS

TODAY APPOINTMENT

Time	Event

SLEEP

MOOD

WATER INTAKE

Total :

EXERCISE

Total Minutes

Total Steps

THINGS TO GET DONE TODAY

MEAL TRACKER

Breakfast

Lunch

Dinner

Snack

REMINDER

TODAY I'M GRATEFUL FOR

NOTES

MONEY TRACKER

Money In

Money Out

DAILY PLANNER

DATE S M T W T F S

TODAY'S GOALS

WATER INTAKE

Total :

MEAL TRACKER

Breakfast

Lunch

Dinner

Snack

MONEY TRACKER

Money In	Money Out

TODAY APPOINTMENT

Time	Event

THINGS TO GET DONE TODAY

TODAY I'M GRATEFUL FOR

SLEEP

MOOD

EXERCISE

Total Minutes

Total Steps

REMINDER

NOTES

DAILY PLANNER

DATE

S M T W T F S

TODAY'S GOALS

TODAY APPOINTMENT

Time	Event

SLEEP

MOOD

WATER INTAKE

Total :

EXERCISE

Total Minutes

Total Steps

MEAL TRACKER

Breakfast

Lunch

Dinner

Snack

THINGS TO GET DONE TODAY

REMINDER

TODAY I'M GRATEFUL FOR

NOTES

MONEY TRACKER

Money In	Money Out

DAILY PLANNER

DATE S M T W T F S

TODAY'S GOALS

TODAY APPOINTMENT

Time	Event

SLEEP

MOOD

WATER INTAKE

Total :

EXERCISE

Total Minutes

Total Steps

MEAL TRACKER

Breakfast

Lunch

Dinner

Snack

THINGS TO GET DONE TODAY

REMINDER

MONEY TRACKER

Money In

Money Out

TODAY I'M GRATEFUL FOR

NOTES

WEEKLY PLANNER

WEEK OF

MOTIVATION

MON

TUE

WED

THUR

FRI

SAT

SUN

TO-DO

TOP PRIORITIES

NOTES

DAILY PLANNER

DATE S M T W T F S

TODAY'S GOALS

TODAY APPOINTMENT

Time	Event

SLEEP

MOOD

WATER INTAKE

Total :

EXERCISE

Total Minutes

Total Steps

THINGS TO GET DONE TODAY

MEAL TRACKER

Breakfast

Lunch

Dinner

Snack

REMINDER

TODAY I'M GRATEFUL FOR

NOTES

MONEY TRACKER

Money In	Money Out

DAILY PLANNER

DATE

S M T W T F S

TODAY'S GOALS

TODAY APPOINTMENT

Time	Event

SLEEP

MOOD

WATER INTAKE

Total :

EXERCISE

Total Minutes

Total Steps

THINGS TO GET DONE TODAY

MEAL TRACKER

Breakfast

Lunch

Dinner

Snack

REMINDER

TODAY I'M GRATEFUL FOR

NOTES

MONEY TRACKER

Money In	Money Out

DAILY PLANNER

DATE — S M T W T F S

TODAY'S GOALS

TODAY APPOINTMENT

Time	Event

SLEEP

MOOD

WATER INTAKE

Total :

EXERCISE

Total Minutes

Total Steps

MEAL TRACKER

Breakfast

Lunch

Dinner

Snack

THINGS TO GET DONE TODAY

REMINDER

TODAY I'M GRATEFUL FOR

NOTES

MONEY TRACKER

Money In	Money Out

DAILY PLANNER

DATE

S M T W T F S

TODAY'S GOALS

TODAY APPOINTMENT

Time	Event

SLEEP

MOOD

WATER INTAKE

Total :

EXERCISE

Total Minutes

Total Steps

MEAL TRACKER

Breakfast

Lunch

Dinner

Snack

THINGS TO GET DONE TODAY

REMINDER

TODAY I'M GRATEFUL FOR

NOTES

MONEY TRACKER

Money In	Money Out

DAILY PLANNER

DATE S M T W T F S

TODAY'S GOALS

TODAY APPOINTMENT

Time	Event

SLEEP

MOOD

WATER INTAKE

Total :

EXERCISE

Total Minutes

Total Steps

MEAL TRACKER

Breakfast

Lunch

Dinner

Snack

THINGS TO GET DONE TODAY

REMINDER

TODAY I'M GRATEFUL FOR

NOTES

MONEY TRACKER

Money In	Money Out

DAILY PLANNER

DATE

S M T W T F S

TODAY'S GOALS

TODAY APPOINTMENT

Time	Event

SLEEP

MOOD

WATER INTAKE

Total :

EXERCISE

Total Minutes

Total Steps

THINGS TO GET DONE TODAY

MEAL TRACKER

Breakfast

Lunch

Dinner

Snack

REMINDER

TODAY I'M GRATEFUL FOR

NOTES

MONEY TRACKER

Money In	Money Out

DAILY PLANNER

DATE S M T W T F S

TODAY'S GOALS

TODAY APPOINTMENT

Time	Event

SLEEP

MOOD

WATER INTAKE

Total :

EXERCISE

Total Minutes

Total Steps

MEAL TRACKER

Breakfast

Lunch

Dinner

Snack

THINGS TO GET DONE TODAY

REMINDER

TODAY I'M GRATEFUL FOR

NOTES

MONEY TRACKER

Money In	Money Out

DAILY PLANNER

DATE

S M T W T F S

TODAY'S GOALS

TODAY APPOINTMENT

Time	Event

SLEEP

MOOD

WATER INTAKE

Total :

EXERCISE

Total Minutes

Total Steps

MEAL TRACKER

Breakfast

Lunch

Dinner

Snack

THINGS TO GET DONE TODAY

REMINDER

TODAY I'M GRATEFUL FOR

NOTES

MONEY TRACKER

Money In	Money Out

DAILY PLANNER

DATE S M T W T F S

TODAY'S GOALS

TODAY APPOINTMENT

Time	Event

SLEEP

MOOD

WATER INTAKE

Total :

EXERCISE

Total Minutes

Total Steps

MEAL TRACKER

Breakfast

Lunch

Dinner

Snack

THINGS TO GET DONE TODAY

REMINDER

MONEY TRACKER

Money In

Money Out

TODAY I'M GRATEFUL FOR

NOTES

DAILY PLANNER

DATE

S M T W T F S

TODAY'S GOALS

TODAY APPOINTMENT

Time	Event

SLEEP

MOOD

WATER INTAKE

Total :

EXERCISE

Total Minutes

Total Steps

THINGS TO GET DONE TODAY

MEAL TRACKER

Breakfast

Lunch

Dinner

Snack

REMINDER

TODAY I'M GRATEFUL FOR

NOTES

MONEY TRACKER

Money In	Money Out

NOTES

AUGUST

Monday	Tuesday	Wednesday	Thursday

To-Do

Affirmations For The month

Important Dates

Habits

To start	To stop

What do I love about myself?

Friday	Saturday	Sunday

Self-Care Activities

Main Goals

Appointments

Notes

AUGUST BUDGET

Source Of Income	Amount
	$
	$
	$
Total Income	$

Expenses

Date	Bills	Budget	Actual
		$	$
		$	$
		$	$
		$	$
		$	$
		$	$
		$	$
		$	$
		$	$
		$	$
Total		$	$

Date	Groceries	Budget	Actual
		$	$
		$	$
		$	$
		$	$
		$	$
		$	$
		$	$
Total		$	$

Date	Trasportation	Budget	Actual
		$	$
		$	$
		$	$
Total		$	$

Date	Shopping	Budget	Actual
		$	$
		$	$
		$	$
		$	$
		$	$
		$	$
Total		$	$

Date	Entertainment	Budget	Actual
		$	$
		$	$
		$	$
Total		$	$

Date	Fees & Charges	Budget	Actual
		$	$
		$	$
		$	$
Total		$	$

Date	Saving	Goal	Needed
		$	$
		$	$
		$	$
Total		$	$

TIME TRACKER

Use a green marker to highlight the hours you are focused and working on your goals. Over the course of the month – revisit and see what your productivity looks like.

DATE	AM	PM
1	1 2 3 4 5 6 7 8 9 10 11 12	1 2 3 4 5 6 7 8 9 10 11 12
2	1 2 3 4 5 6 7 8 9 10 11 12	1 2 3 4 5 6 7 8 9 10 11 12
3	1 2 3 4 5 6 7 8 9 10 11 12	1 2 3 4 5 6 7 8 9 10 11 12
4	1 2 3 4 5 6 7 8 9 10 11 12	1 2 3 4 5 6 7 8 9 10 11 12
5	1 2 3 4 5 6 7 8 9 10 11 12	1 2 3 4 5 6 7 8 9 10 11 12
6	1 2 3 4 5 6 7 8 9 10 11 12	1 2 3 4 5 6 7 8 9 10 11 12
7	1 2 3 4 5 6 7 8 9 10 11 12	1 2 3 4 5 6 7 8 9 10 11 12
8	1 2 3 4 5 6 7 8 9 10 11 12	1 2 3 4 5 6 7 8 9 10 11 12
9	1 2 3 4 5 6 7 8 9 10 11 12	1 2 3 4 5 6 7 8 9 10 11 12
10	1 2 3 4 5 6 7 8 9 10 11 12	1 2 3 4 5 6 7 8 9 10 11 12
11	1 2 3 4 5 6 7 8 9 10 11 12	1 2 3 4 5 6 7 8 9 10 11 12
12	1 2 3 4 5 6 7 8 9 10 11 12	1 2 3 4 5 6 7 8 9 10 11 12
13	1 2 3 4 5 6 7 8 9 10 11 12	1 2 3 4 5 6 7 8 9 10 11 12
14	1 2 3 4 5 6 7 8 9 10 11 12	1 2 3 4 5 6 7 8 9 10 11 12
15	1 2 3 4 5 6 7 8 9 10 11 12	1 2 3 4 5 6 7 8 9 10 11 12
16	1 2 3 4 5 6 7 8 9 10 11 12	1 2 3 4 5 6 7 8 9 10 11 12
17	1 2 3 4 5 6 7 8 9 10 11 12	1 2 3 4 5 6 7 8 9 10 11 12
18	1 2 3 4 5 6 7 8 9 10 11 12	1 2 3 4 5 6 7 8 9 10 11 12
19	1 2 3 4 5 6 7 8 9 10 11 12	1 2 3 4 5 6 7 8 9 10 11 12
20	1 2 3 4 5 6 7 8 9 10 11 12	1 2 3 4 5 6 7 8 9 10 11 12
21	1 2 3 4 5 6 7 8 9 10 11 12	1 2 3 4 5 6 7 8 9 10 11 12
22	1 2 3 4 5 6 7 8 9 10 11 12	1 2 3 4 5 6 7 8 9 10 11 12
23	1 2 3 4 5 6 7 8 9 10 11 12	1 2 3 4 5 6 7 8 9 10 11 12
24	1 2 3 4 5 6 7 8 9 10 11 12	1 2 3 4 5 6 7 8 9 10 11 12
25	1 2 3 4 5 6 7 8 9 10 11 12	1 2 3 4 5 6 7 8 9 10 11 12
26	1 2 3 4 5 6 7 8 9 10 11 12	1 2 3 4 5 6 7 8 9 10 11 12
27	1 2 3 4 5 6 7 8 9 10 11 12	1 2 3 4 5 6 7 8 9 10 11 12
28	1 2 3 4 5 6 7 8 9 10 11 12	1 2 3 4 5 6 7 8 9 10 11 12
29	1 2 3 4 5 6 7 8 9 10 11 12	1 2 3 4 5 6 7 8 9 10 11 12
30	1 2 3 4 5 6 7 8 9 10 11 12	1 2 3 4 5 6 7 8 9 10 11 12
31	1 2 3 4 5 6 7 8 9 10 11 12	1 2 3 4 5 6 7 8 9 10 11 12

CLIENT INFORMATION

Name
Phone
Email
Website
Address
Billing Adress
City
State Zip
D.O.B
Business Hours

Additional Information

Name
Phone
Email
Website
Address
Billing Adress
City
State Zip
D.O.B
Business Hours

Additional Information

Name
Phone
Email
Website
Address
Billing Adress
City
State Zip
D.O.B
Business Hours

Additional Information

Name
Phone
Email
Website
Address
Billing Adress
City
State Zip
D.O.B
Business Hours

Additional Information

CLIENT INFORMATION

Name
Phone
Email
Website
Address
Billing Adress
City
State Zip
D.O.B
Business Hours

Additional Information

Name
Phone
Email
Website
Address
Billing Adress
City
State Zip
D.O.B
Business Hours

Additional Information

Name
Phone
Email
Website
Address
Billing Adress
City
State Zip
D.O.B
Business Hours

Additional Information

Name
Phone
Email
Website
Address
Billing Adress
City
State Zip
D.O.B
Business Hours

Additional Information

MEETING NOTES

SUBJECT	DATE	TIME

AGENDA

ATTENDEES

-
-
-
-
-

IMPORTANT NOTES

SUBJECT	DATE	TIME

AGENDA

ATTENDEES

-
-
-
-
-

IMPORTANT NOTES

MEETING NOTES

SUBJECT	DATE	TIME

AGENDA

ATTENDEES

-
-
-
-
-

IMPORTANT NOTES

SUBJECT	DATE	TIME

AGENDA

ATTENDEES

-
-
-
-
-

IMPORTANT NOTES

AUGUST SELF-CARE

Write a self-care activity and tick off each time you do self-care act.

ACTIVITIES	CHECKLIST
	1 2 3 4 5 6 7 8 9 10 11 12 13 14 15 16 17 18 19 20 21 22 23 24 25 26 27 28 29 30 31
	1 2 3 4 5 6 7 8 9 10 11 12 13 14 15 16 17 18 19 20 21 22 23 24 25 26 27 28 29 30 31
	1 2 3 4 5 6 7 8 9 10 11 12 13 14 15 16 17 18 19 20 21 22 23 24 25 26 27 28 29 30 31
	1 2 3 4 5 6 7 8 9 10 11 12 13 14 15 16 17 18 19 20 21 22 23 24 25 26 27 28 29 30 31
	1 2 3 4 5 6 7 8 9 10 11 12 13 14 15 16 17 18 19 20 21 22 23 24 25 26 27 28 29 30 31
	1 2 3 4 5 6 7 8 9 10 11 12 13 14 15 16 17 18 19 20 21 22 23 24 25 26 27 28 29 30 31
	1 2 3 4 5 6 7 8 9 10 11 12 13 14 15 16 17 18 19 20 21 22 23 24 25 26 27 28 29 30 31
	1 2 3 4 5 6 7 8 9 10 11 12 13 14 15 16 17 18 19 20 21 22 23 24 25 26 27 28 29 30 31
	1 2 3 4 5 6 7 8 9 10 11 12 13 14 15 16 17 18 19 20 21 22 23 24 25 26 27 28 29 30 31
	1 2 3 4 5 6 7 8 9 10 11 12 13 14 15 16 17 18 19 20 21 22 23 24 25 26 27 28 29 30 31

REFLECTION

HOW WILL YOU RATE THIS MONTH? ☆ ☆ ☆ ☆ ☆ ☆ ☆ ☆ ☆ ☆

MONTHLY WINS	HOW DOES IT MAKE ME FEEL?
•	•
•	•
•	•
•	•

CHALLENGES	HOW CAN I IMPROVE IT?
•	•
•	•
•	•
•	•

ACCOMPLISHED GOALS	UNACCOMPLISHED GOALS	GOALS NEXT MONTH

HABITS RETAINED	HABITS ELIMINATED	NEW HABITS DEVELOPED

THREE THINGS THAT I AM MOST GRATEFUL FOR THIS MONTH

1	2	3

TWO LIFE LESSONS I LEARNED THIS MONTH

1	2

ONE WORD THAT BEST DESCRIBES THIS MONTH

WEEKLY PLANNER

WEEK OF	
MOTIVATION	

MON	
TUE	
WED	
THUR	
FRI	
SAT	
SUN	

TO-DO

TOP PRIORITIES

NOTES

DAILY PLANNER

DATE

S M T W T F S

TODAY'S GOALS

TODAY APPOINTMENT

Time	Event

SLEEP

MOOD

WATER INTAKE

Total :

EXERCISE

Total Minutes

Total Steps

THINGS TO GET DONE TODAY

MEAL TRACKER

Breakfast

Lunch

Dinner

Snack

REMINDER

TODAY I'M GRATEFUL FOR

NOTES

MONEY TRACKER

Money In	Money Out

DAILY PLANNER

DATE

S M T W T F S

TODAY'S GOALS

TODAY APPOINTMENT

Time	Event

SLEEP

MOOD

WATER INTAKE

Total :

EXERCISE

Total Minutes

Total Steps

THINGS TO GET DONE TODAY

MEAL TRACKER

Breakfast

Lunch

Dinner

Snack

REMINDER

TODAY I'M GRATEFUL FOR

NOTES

MONEY TRACKER

Money In	Money Out

DAILY PLANNER

DATE S M T W T F S

TODAY'S GOALS

TODAY APPOINTMENT

Time	Event

SLEEP

MOOD

WATER INTAKE

Total :

EXERCISE

Total Minutes

Total Steps

THINGS TO GET DONE TODAY

MEAL TRACKER

Breakfast

Lunch

Dinner

Snack

REMINDER

MONEY TRACKER

Money In	Money Out

TODAY I'M GRATEFUL FOR

NOTES

DAILY PLANNER

DATE

S M T W T F S

TODAY'S GOALS

TODAY APPOINTMENT

Time	Event

SLEEP

MOOD

WATER INTAKE

Total :

EXERCISE

Total Minutes

Total Steps

THINGS TO GET DONE TODAY

MEAL TRACKER

Breakfast

Lunch

Dinner

Snack

REMINDER

TODAY I'M GRATEFUL FOR

NOTES

MONEY TRACKER

Money In	Money Out

DAILY PLANNER

DATE S M T W T F S

TODAY'S GOALS

TODAY APPOINTMENT

Time	Event

SLEEP

MOOD

WATER INTAKE

Total :

EXERCISE

Total Minutes

Total Steps

MEAL TRACKER

Breakfast

Lunch

Dinner

Snack

THINGS TO GET DONE TODAY

REMINDER

TODAY I'M GRATEFUL FOR

NOTES

MONEY TRACKER

Money In	Money Out

DAILY PLANNER

DATE

S M T W T F S

TODAY'S GOALS

TODAY APPOINTMENT

Time	Event

SLEEP

MOOD

WATER INTAKE

Total :

EXERCISE

Total Minutes

Total Steps

THINGS TO GET DONE TODAY

MEAL TRACKER

Breakfast

Lunch

Dinner

Snack

REMINDER

TODAY I'M GRATEFUL FOR

NOTES

MONEY TRACKER

Money In	Money Out

DAILY PLANNER

DATE S M T W T F S

TODAY'S GOALS

TODAY APPOINTMENT

Time	Event

SLEEP

MOOD

WATER INTAKE

Total :

EXERCISE

Total Minutes

Total Steps

MEAL TRACKER

Breakfast

Lunch

Dinner

Snack

THINGS TO GET DONE TODAY

REMINDER

MONEY TRACKER

Money In

Money Out

TODAY I'M GRATEFUL FOR

NOTES

WEEKLY PLANNER

WEEK OF

MOTIVATION

MON

TUE

WED

THUR

FRI

SAT

SUN

TO-DO

TOP PRIORITIES

NOTES

DAILY PLANNER

DATE S M T W T F S

TODAY'S GOALS

TODAY APPOINTMENT

Time	Event

SLEEP

MOOD

WATER INTAKE

Total :

EXERCISE

Total Minutes

Total Steps

MEAL TRACKER

Breakfast

Lunch

Dinner

Snack

THINGS TO GET DONE TODAY

REMINDER

TODAY I'M GRATEFUL FOR

NOTES

MONEY TRACKER

Money In	Money Out

DAILY PLANNER

DATE

S M T W T F S

TODAY'S GOALS

TODAY APPOINTMENT

Time	Event

SLEEP

MOOD

WATER INTAKE

Total :

EXERCISE

Total Minutes

Total Steps

THINGS TO GET DONE TODAY

MEAL TRACKER

Breakfast

Lunch

Dinner

Snack

REMINDER

TODAY I'M GRATEFUL FOR

NOTES

MONEY TRACKER

Money In	Money Out

DAILY PLANNER

DATE S M T W T F S

TODAY'S GOALS

TODAY APPOINTMENT

Time	Event

SLEEP

MOOD

WATER INTAKE

Total :

EXERCISE

Total Minutes

Total Steps

THINGS TO GET DONE TODAY

MEAL TRACKER

Breakfast

Lunch

Dinner

Snack

REMINDER

TODAY I'M GRATEFUL FOR

NOTES

MONEY TRACKER

Money In

Money Out

DAILY PLANNER

DATE

S M T W T F S

TODAY'S GOALS

TODAY APPOINTMENT

Time	Event

SLEEP

MOOD

WATER INTAKE

Total :

EXERCISE

Total Minutes

Total Steps

MEAL TRACKER

Breakfast

Lunch

Dinner

Snack

THINGS TO GET DONE TODAY

REMINDER

TODAY I'M GRATEFUL FOR

NOTES

MONEY TRACKER

Money In	Money Out

DAILY PLANNER

DATE S M T W T F S

TODAY'S GOALS

TODAY APPOINTMENT

Time	Event

SLEEP

MOOD

WATER INTAKE

Total :

EXERCISE

Total Minutes

Total Steps

MEAL TRACKER

Breakfast

Lunch

Dinner

Snack

THINGS TO GET DONE TODAY

REMINDER

TODAY I'M GRATEFUL FOR

NOTES

MONEY TRACKER

Money In	Money Out

DAILY PLANNER

DATE

S M T W T F S

TODAY'S GOALS

TODAY APPOINTMENT

Time	Event

SLEEP

MOOD

WATER INTAKE

Total :

EXERCISE

Total Minutes

Total Steps

THINGS TO GET DONE TODAY

MEAL TRACKER

Breakfast

Lunch

Dinner

Snack

REMINDER

TODAY I'M GRATEFUL FOR

NOTES

MONEY TRACKER

Money In	Money Out

DAILY PLANNER

DATE S M T W T F S

TODAY'S GOALS

TODAY APPOINTMENT

Time	Event

SLEEP

MOOD

WATER INTAKE

Total :

EXERCISE

Total Minutes

Total Steps

THINGS TO GET DONE TODAY

MEAL TRACKER

Breakfast

Lunch

Dinner

Snack

REMINDER

MONEY TRACKER

Money In

Money Out

TODAY I'M GRATEFUL FOR

NOTES

WEEKLY PLANNER

WEEK OF

MOTIVATION

MON

TUE

WED

THUR

FRI

SAT

SUN

TO-DO

TOP PRIORITIES

NOTES

DAILY PLANNER

DATE S M T W T F S

TODAY'S GOALS

TODAY APPOINTMENT

Time	Event

SLEEP

MOOD

WATER INTAKE

Total :

EXERCISE

Total Minutes

Total Steps

MEAL TRACKER

Breakfast

Lunch

Dinner

Snack

THINGS TO GET DONE TODAY

REMINDER

MONEY TRACKER

Money In	Money Out

TODAY I'M GRATEFUL FOR

NOTES

DAILY PLANNER

DATE

S M T W T F S

TODAY'S GOALS

TODAY APPOINTMENT

Time	Event

SLEEP

MOOD

WATER INTAKE

Total :

EXERCISE

Total Minutes

Total Steps

THINGS TO GET DONE TODAY

MEAL TRACKER

Breakfast

Lunch

Dinner

Snack

REMINDER

TODAY I'M GRATEFUL FOR

NOTES

MONEY TRACKER

Money In	Money Out

DAILY PLANNER

DATE S M T W T F S

TODAY'S GOALS

TODAY APPOINTMENT

Time	Event

SLEEP

MOOD

WATER INTAKE

Total :

EXERCISE

Total Minutes

Total Steps

MEAL TRACKER

Breakfast

Lunch

Dinner

Snack

THINGS TO GET DONE TODAY

REMINDER

TODAY I'M GRATEFUL FOR

NOTES

MONEY TRACKER

Money In	Money Out

DAILY PLANNER

DATE

S M T W T F S

TODAY'S GOALS

TODAY APPOINTMENT

Time	Event

SLEEP

MOOD

WATER INTAKE

Total :

EXERCISE

Total Minutes

Total Steps

THINGS TO GET DONE TODAY

MEAL TRACKER

Breakfast

Lunch

Dinner

Snack

REMINDER

TODAY I'M GRATEFUL FOR

NOTES

MONEY TRACKER

Money In	Money Out

DAILY PLANNER

DATE S M T W T F S

TODAY'S GOALS

TODAY APPOINTMENT

Time	Event

SLEEP

MOOD

WATER INTAKE

Total :

EXERCISE

Total Minutes

Total Steps

MEAL TRACKER

Breakfast

Lunch

Dinner

Snack

THINGS TO GET DONE TODAY

REMINDER

TODAY I'M GRATEFUL FOR

NOTES

MONEY TRACKER

Money In

Money Out

DAILY PLANNER

DATE

S M T W T F S

TODAY'S GOALS

TODAY APPOINTMENT

Time	Event

SLEEP

MOOD

WATER INTAKE

Total :

EXERCISE

Total Minutes

Total Steps

THINGS TO GET DONE TODAY

MEAL TRACKER

Breakfast

Lunch

Dinner

Snack

REMINDER

TODAY I'M GRATEFUL FOR

NOTES

MONEY TRACKER

Money In	Money Out

DAILY PLANNER

DATE S M T W T F S

TODAY'S GOALS

TODAY APPOINTMENT

Time	Event

SLEEP

MOOD

WATER INTAKE

Total :

EXERCISE

Total Minutes

Total Steps

MEAL TRACKER

Breakfast

Lunch

Dinner

Snack

THINGS TO GET DONE TODAY

REMINDER

TODAY I'M GRATEFUL FOR

NOTES

MONEY TRACKER

Money In	Money Out

WEEKLY PLANNER

WEEK OF	
MOTIVATION	

MON	
TUE	
WED	
THUR	
FRI	
SAT	
SUN	

TO-DO

TOP PRIORITIES

NOTES

DAILY PLANNER

DATE S M T W T F S

TODAY'S GOALS

TODAY APPOINTMENT

Time	Event

SLEEP

MOOD

WATER INTAKE

Total :

EXERCISE

Total Minutes

Total Steps

THINGS TO GET DONE TODAY

MEAL TRACKER

Breakfast

Lunch

Dinner

Snack

REMINDER

TODAY I'M GRATEFUL FOR

MONEY TRACKER

Money In	Money Out

NOTES

DAILY PLANNER

DATE

S M T W T F S

TODAY'S GOALS

TODAY APPOINTMENT

Time	Event

SLEEP

MOOD

WATER INTAKE

Total :

EXERCISE

Total Minutes

Total Steps

THINGS TO GET DONE TODAY

MEAL TRACKER

Breakfast

Lunch

Dinner

Snack

REMINDER

TODAY I'M GRATEFUL FOR

NOTES

MONEY TRACKER

Money In	Money Out

DAILY PLANNER

DATE S M T W T F S

TODAY'S GOALS

TODAY APPOINTMENT

Time	Event

SLEEP

MOOD

WATER INTAKE

Total :

EXERCISE

Total Minutes

Total Steps

MEAL TRACKER

Breakfast

Lunch

Dinner

Snack

THINGS TO GET DONE TODAY

REMINDER

TODAY I'M GRATEFUL FOR

NOTES

MONEY TRACKER

Money In

Money Out

DAILY PLANNER

DATE

S M T W T F S

TODAY'S GOALS

TODAY APPOINTMENT

Time	Event

SLEEP

MOOD

WATER INTAKE

Total :

EXERCISE

Total Minutes

Total Steps

THINGS TO GET DONE TODAY

MEAL TRACKER

Breakfast

Lunch

Dinner

Snack

REMINDER

TODAY I'M GRATEFUL FOR

NOTES

MONEY TRACKER

Money In	Money Out

DAILY PLANNER

DATE S M T W T F S

TODAY'S GOALS

TODAY APPOINTMENT

Time	Event

SLEEP

MOOD

WATER INTAKE

Total :

EXERCISE

Total Minutes

Total Steps

MEAL TRACKER

Breakfast

Lunch

Dinner

Snack

THINGS TO GET DONE TODAY

REMINDER

MONEY TRACKER

Money In	Money Out

TODAY I'M GRATEFUL FOR

NOTES

DAILY PLANNER

DATE

S M T W T F S

TODAY'S GOALS

TODAY APPOINTMENT

Time	Event

SLEEP

MOOD

WATER INTAKE

Total :

EXERCISE

Total Minutes

Total Steps

MEAL TRACKER

Breakfast

Lunch

Dinner

Snack

THINGS TO GET DONE TODAY

REMINDER

MONEY TRACKER

Money In	Money Out

TODAY I'M GRATEFUL FOR

NOTES

DAILY PLANNER

DATE S M T W T F S

TODAY'S GOALS

TODAY APPOINTMENT

Time	Event

SLEEP

MOOD

WATER INTAKE

Total :

EXERCISE

Total Minutes

Total Steps

THINGS TO GET DONE TODAY

MEAL TRACKER

Breakfast

Lunch

Dinner

Snack

REMINDER

TODAY I'M GRATEFUL FOR

NOTES

MONEY TRACKER

Money In	Money Out

DAILY PLANNER

DATE

S M T W T F S

TODAY'S GOALS

TODAY APPOINTMENT

Time	Event

SLEEP

MOOD

WATER INTAKE

Total :

EXERCISE

Total Minutes

Total Steps

MEAL TRACKER

Breakfast

Lunch

Dinner

Snack

THINGS TO GET DONE TODAY

REMINDER

TODAY I'M GRATEFUL FOR

NOTES

MONEY TRACKER

Money In	Money Out

DAILY PLANNER

DATE S M T W T F S

TODAY'S GOALS

TODAY APPOINTMENT

Time	Event

SLEEP

MOOD

WATER INTAKE

Total :

EXERCISE

Total Minutes

Total Steps

MEAL TRACKER

Breakfast

Lunch

Dinner

Snack

THINGS TO GET DONE TODAY

REMINDER

MONEY TRACKER

Money In	Money Out

TODAY I'M GRATEFUL FOR

NOTES

DAILY PLANNER

DATE

S M T W T F S

TODAY'S GOALS

TODAY APPOINTMENT

Time	Event

SLEEP

MOOD

WATER INTAKE

Total :

EXERCISE

Total Minutes

Total Steps

THINGS TO GET DONE TODAY

MEAL TRACKER

Breakfast

Lunch

Dinner

Snack

REMINDER

MONEY TRACKER

Money In

Money Out

TODAY I'M GRATEFUL FOR

NOTES

NOTES

SEPTEMBER

Monday	Tuesday	Wednesday	Thursday

To-Do

Affirmations For The month

Important Dates

Habits

To start	To stop
•	•
•	•
•	•

What do I loveabout myself?

Friday	Saturday	Sunday

Self-Care Activities

Main Goals

Appointments

Notes

SEPTEMBER BUDGET

Source Of Income	Amount
	$
	$
	$
Total Income	$

Expenses

Date	Bills	Budget	Actual
		$	$
		$	$
		$	$
		$	$
		$	$
		$	$
		$	$
		$	$
		$	$
		$	$
Total		$	$

Date	Groceries	Budget	Actual
		$	$
		$	$
		$	$
		$	$
		$	$
		$	$
		$	$
Total		$	$

Date	Transportation	Budget	Actual
		$	$
		$	$
		$	$
Total		$	$

Date	Shopping	Budget	Actual
		$	$
		$	$
		$	$
		$	$
		$	$
		$	$
Total		$	$

Date	Entertainment	Budget	Actual
		$	$
		$	$
		$	$
Total		$	$

Date	Fees & Charges	Budget	Actual
		$	$
		$	$
		$	$
Total		$	$

Date	Saving	Goal	Needed
		$	$
		$	$
		$	$
Total		$	$

TIME TRACKER

Use a green marker to highlight the hours you are focused and working on your goals. Over the course of the month – revisit and see what your productivity looks like.

DATE	AM												PM											
1	1	2	3	4	5	6	7	8	9	10	11	12	1	2	3	4	5	6	7	8	9	10	11	12
2	1	2	3	4	5	6	7	8	9	10	11	12	1	2	3	4	5	6	7	8	9	10	11	12
3	1	2	3	4	5	6	7	8	9	10	11	12	1	2	3	4	5	6	7	8	9	10	11	12
4	1	2	3	4	5	6	7	8	9	10	11	12	1	2	3	4	5	6	7	8	9	10	11	12
5	1	2	3	4	5	6	7	8	9	10	11	12	1	2	3	4	5	6	7	8	9	10	11	12
6	1	2	3	4	5	6	7	8	9	10	11	12	1	2	3	4	5	6	7	8	9	10	11	12
7	1	2	3	4	5	6	7	8	9	10	11	12	1	2	3	4	5	6	7	8	9	10	11	12
8	1	2	3	4	5	6	7	8	9	10	11	12	1	2	3	4	5	6	7	8	9	10	11	12
9	1	2	3	4	5	6	7	8	9	10	11	12	1	2	3	4	5	6	7	8	9	10	11	12
10	1	2	3	4	5	6	7	8	9	10	11	12	1	2	3	4	5	6	7	8	9	10	11	12
11	1	2	3	4	5	6	7	8	9	10	11	12	1	2	3	4	5	6	7	8	9	10	11	12
12	1	2	3	4	5	6	7	8	9	10	11	12	1	2	3	4	5	6	7	8	9	10	11	12
13	1	2	3	4	5	6	7	8	9	10	11	12	1	2	3	4	5	6	7	8	9	10	11	12
14	1	2	3	4	5	6	7	8	9	10	11	12	1	2	3	4	5	6	7	8	9	10	11	12
15	1	2	3	4	5	6	7	8	9	10	11	12	1	2	3	4	5	6	7	8	9	10	11	12
16	1	2	3	4	5	6	7	8	9	10	11	12	1	2	3	4	5	6	7	8	9	10	11	12
17	1	2	3	4	5	6	7	8	9	10	11	12	1	2	3	4	5	6	7	8	9	10	11	12
18	1	2	3	4	5	6	7	8	9	10	11	12	1	2	3	4	5	6	7	8	9	10	11	12
19	1	2	3	4	5	6	7	8	9	10	11	12	1	2	3	4	5	6	7	8	9	10	11	12
20	1	2	3	4	5	6	7	8	9	10	11	12	1	2	3	4	5	6	7	8	9	10	11	12
21	1	2	3	4	5	6	7	8	9	10	11	12	1	2	3	4	5	6	7	8	9	10	11	12
22	1	2	3	4	5	6	7	8	9	10	11	12	1	2	3	4	5	6	7	8	9	10	11	12
23	1	2	3	4	5	6	7	8	9	10	11	12	1	2	3	4	5	6	7	8	9	10	11	12
24	1	2	3	4	5	6	7	8	9	10	11	12	1	2	3	4	5	6	7	8	9	10	11	12
25	1	2	3	4	5	6	7	8	9	10	11	12	1	2	3	4	5	6	7	8	9	10	11	12
26	1	2	3	4	5	6	7	8	9	10	11	12	1	2	3	4	5	6	7	8	9	10	11	12
27	1	2	3	4	5	6	7	8	9	10	11	12	1	2	3	4	5	6	7	8	9	10	11	12
28	1	2	3	4	5	6	7	8	9	10	11	12	1	2	3	4	5	6	7	8	9	10	11	12
29	1	2	3	4	5	6	7	8	9	10	11	12	1	2	3	4	5	6	7	8	9	10	11	12
30	1	2	3	4	5	6	7	8	9	10	11	12	1	2	3	4	5	6	7	8	9	10	11	12
31	1	2	3	4	5	6	7	8	9	10	11	12	1	2	3	4	5	6	7	8	9	10	11	12

CLIENT INFORMATION

Name
Phone
Email
Website
Address
Billing Adress
City
State Zip
D.O.B
Business Hours

Additional Information

Name
Phone
Email
Website
Address
Billing Adress
City
State Zip
D.O.B
Business Hours

Additional Information

Name
Phone
Email
Website
Address
Billing Adress
City
State Zip
D.O.B
Business Hours

Additional Information

Name
Phone
Email
Website
Address
Billing Adress
City
State Zip
D.O.B
Business Hours

Additional Information

CLIENT INFORMATION

Name
Phone
Email
Website
Address
Billing Adress
City
State Zip
D.O.B
Business Hours

Additional Information

Name
Phone
Email
Website
Address
Billing Adress
City
State Zip
D.O.B
Business Hours

Additional Information

Name
Phone
Email
Website
Address
Billing Adress
City
State Zip
D.O.B
Business Hours

Additional Information

Name
Phone
Email
Website
Address
Billing Adress
City
State Zip
D.O.B
Business Hours

Additional Information

MEETING NOTES

SUBJECT	DATE	TIME

AGENDA

ATTENDEES

IMPORTANT NOTES

SUBJECT	DATE	TIME

AGENDA

ATTENDEES

IMPORTANT NOTES

MEETING NOTES

SUBJECT	DATE	TIME

AGENDA

ATTENDEES

-
-
-
-
-

IMPORTANT NOTES

SUBJECT	DATE	TIME

AGENDA

ATTENDEES

-
-
-
-
-

IMPORTANT NOTES

SEPTEMBER SELF-CARE

Write a self-care activity and tick off each time you do self-care act.

ACTIVITIES	CHECKLIST
	1 2 3 4 5 6 7 8 9 10 11 12 13 14 15 16 17 18 19 20 21 22 23 24 25 26 27 28 29 30 31
	1 2 3 4 5 6 7 8 9 10 11 12 13 14 15 16 17 18 19 20 21 22 23 24 25 26 27 28 29 30 31
	1 2 3 4 5 6 7 8 9 10 11 12 13 14 15 16 17 18 19 20 21 22 23 24 25 26 27 28 29 30 31
	1 2 3 4 5 6 7 8 9 10 11 12 13 14 15 16 17 18 19 20 21 22 23 24 25 26 27 28 29 30 31
	1 2 3 4 5 6 7 8 9 10 11 12 13 14 15 16 17 18 19 20 21 22 23 24 25 26 27 28 29 30 31
	1 2 3 4 5 6 7 8 9 10 11 12 13 14 15 16 17 18 19 20 21 22 23 24 25 26 27 28 29 30 31
	1 2 3 4 5 6 7 8 9 10 11 12 13 14 15 16 17 18 19 20 21 22 23 24 25 26 27 28 29 30 31
	1 2 3 4 5 6 7 8 9 10 11 12 13 14 15 16 17 18 19 20 21 22 23 24 25 26 27 28 29 30 31
	1 2 3 4 5 6 7 8 9 10 11 12 13 14 15 16 17 18 19 20 21 22 23 24 25 26 27 28 29 30 31
	1 2 3 4 5 6 7 8 9 10 11 12 13 14 15 16 17 18 19 20 21 22 23 24 25 26 27 28 29 30 31

REFLECTION

HOW WILL YOU RATE THIS MONTH? ☆☆☆☆☆☆☆☆☆☆

MONTHLY WINS	HOW DOES IT MAKE ME FEEL?
•	•
•	•
•	•
•	•

CHALLENGES	HOW CAN I IMPROVE IT?
•	•
•	•
•	•
•	•

ACCOMPLISHED GOALS	UNACCOMPLISHED GOALS	GOALS NEXT MONTH

HABITS RETAINED	HABITS ELIMINATED	NEW HABITS DEVELOPED

THREE THINGS THAT I AM MOST GRATEFUL FOR THIS MONTH

1	2	3

TWO LIFE LESSONS I LEARNED THIS MONTH

1	2

ONE WORD THAT BEST DESCRIBES THIS MONTH

WEEKLY PLANNER

WEEK OF

MOTIVATION

MON

TUE

WED

THUR

FRI

SAT

SUN

TO-DO

TOP PRIORITIES

NOTES

DAILY PLANNER

DATE S M T W T F S

TODAY'S GOALS

TODAY APPOINTMENT

Time	Event

SLEEP

MOOD

WATER INTAKE

Total :

EXERCISE

Total Minutes

Total Steps

MEAL TRACKER

Breakfast

Lunch

Dinner

Snack

THINGS TO GET DONE TODAY

REMINDER

TODAY I'M GRATEFUL FOR

NOTES

MONEY TRACKER

Money In	Money Out

DAILY PLANNER

DATE

S M T W T F S

TODAY'S GOALS

TODAY APPOINTMENT

Time	Event

SLEEP

MOOD

WATER INTAKE

Total :

EXERCISE

Total Minutes

Total Steps

THINGS TO GET DONE TODAY

MEAL TRACKER

Breakfast

Lunch

Dinner

Snack

REMINDER

TODAY I'M GRATEFUL FOR

NOTES

MONEY TRACKER

Money In	Money Out

DAILY PLANNER

DATE S M T W T F S

TODAY'S GOALS

TODAY APPOINTMENT

Time	Event

SLEEP

MOOD

WATER INTAKE

Total :

EXERCISE

Total Minutes

Total Steps

MEAL TRACKER

Breakfast

Lunch

Dinner

Snack

THINGS TO GET DONE TODAY

REMINDER

TODAY I'M GRATEFUL FOR

NOTES

MONEY TRACKER

Money In	Money Out

DAILY PLANNER

DATE

S M T W T F S

TODAY'S GOALS

TODAY APPOINTMENT

Time	Event

SLEEP

MOOD

WATER INTAKE

Total :

EXERCISE

Total Minutes

Total Steps

THINGS TO GET DONE TODAY

MEAL TRACKER

Breakfast

Lunch

Dinner

Snack

REMINDER

MONEY TRACKER

Money In	Money Out

TODAY I'M GRATEFUL FOR

NOTES

DAILY PLANNER

DATE S M T W T F S

TODAY'S GOALS

TODAY APPOINTMENT

Time	Event

SLEEP

MOOD

WATER INTAKE

Total :

EXERCISE

Total Minutes

Total Steps

MEAL TRACKER

Breakfast

Lunch

Dinner

Snack

THINGS TO GET DONE TODAY

REMINDER

MONEY TRACKER

Money In

Money Out

TODAY I'M GRATEFUL FOR

NOTES

DAILY PLANNER

DATE

S M T W T F S

TODAY'S GOALS

TODAY APPOINTMENT

Time	Event

SLEEP

MOOD

WATER INTAKE

Total :

EXERCISE

Total Minutes

Total Steps

MEAL TRACKER

Breakfast

Lunch

Dinner

Snack

THINGS TO GET DONE TODAY

REMINDER

TODAY I'M GRATEFUL FOR

NOTES

MONEY TRACKER

Money In	Money Out

DAILY PLANNER

DATE S M T W T F S

TODAY'S GOALS

TODAY APPOINTMENT

Time	Event

SLEEP

MOOD

WATER INTAKE

Total :

EXERCISE

Total Minutes

Total Steps

THINGS TO GET DONE TODAY

MEAL TRACKER

Breakfast

Lunch

Dinner

Snack

REMINDER

MONEY TRACKER

Money In	Money Out

TODAY I'M GRATEFUL FOR

NOTES

WEEKLY PLANNER

WEEK OF

MOTIVATION

MON

TUE

WED

THUR

FRI

SAT

SUN

TO-DO

TOP PRIORITIES

NOTES

DAILY PLANNER

DATE S M T W T F S

TODAY'S GOALS

TODAY APPOINTMENT

Time	Event

SLEEP

MOOD

WATER INTAKE

Total :

EXERCISE

Total Minutes

Total Steps

MEAL TRACKER

Breakfast

Lunch

Dinner

Snack

THINGS TO GET DONE TODAY

REMINDER

TODAY I'M GRATEFUL FOR

NOTES

MONEY TRACKER

Money In	Money Out

DAILY PLANNER

DATE

S M T W T F S

TODAY'S GOALS

TODAY APPOINTMENT

Time	Event

SLEEP

MOOD

WATER INTAKE

Total :

EXERCISE

Total Minutes

Total Steps

THINGS TO GET DONE TODAY

MEAL TRACKER

Breakfast

Lunch

Dinner

Snack

REMINDER

TODAY I'M GRATEFUL FOR

NOTES

MONEY TRACKER

Money In	Money Out

DAILY PLANNER

DATE S M T W T F S

TODAY'S GOALS

TODAY APPOINTMENT

Time	Event

SLEEP

MOOD

WATER INTAKE

Total :

EXERCISE

Total Minutes

Total Steps

MEAL TRACKER

Breakfast

Lunch

Dinner

Snack

THINGS TO GET DONE TODAY

REMINDER

TODAY I'M GRATEFUL FOR

NOTES

MONEY TRACKER

Money In	Money Out

DAILY PLANNER

DATE

S M T W T F S

TODAY'S GOALS

TODAY APPOINTMENT

Time	Event

SLEEP

MOOD

WATER INTAKE

Total :

EXERCISE

Total Minutes

Total Steps

THINGS TO GET DONE TODAY

MEAL TRACKER

Breakfast

Lunch

Dinner

Snack

REMINDER

TODAY I'M GRATEFUL FOR

NOTES

MONEY TRACKER

Money In	Money Out

DAILY PLANNER

DATE S M T W T F S

TODAY'S GOALS

TODAY APPOINTMENT

Time	Event

SLEEP

MOOD

WATER INTAKE

Total :

EXERCISE

Total Minutes

Total Steps

MEAL TRACKER

Breakfast

Lunch

Dinner

Snack

THINGS TO GET DONE TODAY

REMINDER

TODAY I'M GRATEFUL FOR

NOTES

MONEY TRACKER

Money In	Money Out

DAILY PLANNER

DATE

S M T W T F S

TODAY'S GOALS

WATER INTAKE

Total :

MEAL TRACKER

Breakfast

Lunch

Dinner

Snack

MONEY TRACKER

Money In	Money Out

TODAY APPOINTMENT

Time	Event

THINGS TO GET DONE TODAY

TODAY I'M GRATEFUL FOR

SLEEP

MOOD

EXERCISE

Total Minutes

Total Steps

REMINDER

NOTES

DAILY PLANNER

DATE S M T W T F S

TODAY'S GOALS

TODAY APPOINTMENT

Time	Event

SLEEP

MOOD

WATER INTAKE

Total :

EXERCISE

Total Minutes

Total Steps

THINGS TO GET DONE TODAY

MEAL TRACKER

Breakfast

Lunch

Dinner

Snack

REMINDER

TODAY I'M GRATEFUL FOR

NOTES

MONEY TRACKER

Money In	Money Out

WEEKLY PLANNER

WEEK OF

MOTIVATION

MON

TUE

WED

THUR

FRI

SAT

SUN

TO-DO

TOP PRIORITIES

NOTES

DAILY PLANNER

DATE S M T W T F S

TODAY'S GOALS

TODAY APPOINTMENT

Time	Event

SLEEP

MOOD

WATER INTAKE

Total :

EXERCISE

Total Minutes

Total Steps

THINGS TO GET DONE TODAY

MEAL TRACKER

Breakfast

Lunch

Dinner

Snack

REMINDER

TODAY I'M GRATEFUL FOR

NOTES

MONEY TRACKER

Money In	Money Out

DAILY PLANNER

DATE

S M T W T F S

TODAY'S GOALS

TODAY APPOINTMENT

Time	Event

SLEEP

MOOD

WATER INTAKE

Total :

EXERCISE

Total Minutes

Total Steps

THINGS TO GET DONE TODAY

MEAL TRACKER

Breakfast

Lunch

Dinner

Snack

REMINDER

TODAY I'M GRATEFUL FOR

NOTES

MONEY TRACKER

Money In	Money Out

DAILY PLANNER

DATE S M T W T F S

TODAY'S GOALS

TODAY APPOINTMENT

Time	Event

SLEEP

MOOD

WATER INTAKE

Total :

EXERCISE

Total Minutes

Total Steps

THINGS TO GET DONE TODAY

MEAL TRACKER

Breakfast

Lunch

Dinner

Snack

REMINDER

TODAY I'M GRATEFUL FOR

MONEY TRACKER

Money In	Money Out

NOTES

DAILY PLANNER

DATE

S M T W T F S

TODAY'S GOALS

TODAY APPOINTMENT

Time	Event

SLEEP

MOOD

WATER INTAKE

Total :

EXERCISE

Total Minutes

Total Steps

MEAL TRACKER

Breakfast

Lunch

Dinner

Snack

THINGS TO GET DONE TODAY

REMINDER

MONEY TRACKER

Money In

Money Out

TODAY I'M GRATEFUL FOR

NOTES

DAILY PLANNER

DATE S M T W T F S

TODAY'S GOALS

TODAY APPOINTMENT

Time	Event

SLEEP

MOOD

WATER INTAKE

Total :

EXERCISE

Total Minutes

Total Steps

THINGS TO GET DONE TODAY

MEAL TRACKER

Breakfast

Lunch

Dinner

Snack

REMINDER

TODAY I'M GRATEFUL FOR

NOTES

MONEY TRACKER

Money In	Money Out

DAILY PLANNER

DATE

S M T W T F S

TODAY'S GOALS

TODAY APPOINTMENT

Time	Event

SLEEP

MOOD

WATER INTAKE

Total :

EXERCISE

Total Minutes

Total Steps

THINGS TO GET DONE TODAY

MEAL TRACKER

Breakfast

Lunch

Dinner

Snack

REMINDER

TODAY I'M GRATEFUL FOR

NOTES

MONEY TRACKER

Money In	Money Out

DAILY PLANNER

DATE

S M T W T F S

TODAY'S GOALS

TODAY APPOINTMENT

Time	Event

SLEEP

MOOD

WATER INTAKE

Total :

EXERCISE

Total Minutes

Total Steps

MEAL TRACKER

Breakfast

Lunch

Dinner

Snack

THINGS TO GET DONE TODAY

REMINDER

TODAY I'M GRATEFUL FOR

NOTES

MONEY TRACKER

Money In	Money Out

WEEKLY PLANNER

WEEK OF

MOTIVATION

MON

TUE

WED

THUR

FRI

SAT

SUN

TO-DO

TOP PRIORITIES

NOTES

DAILY PLANNER

DATE S M T W T F S

TODAY'S GOALS

TODAY APPOINTMENT

Time	Event

SLEEP

MOOD

WATER INTAKE

Total :

EXERCISE

Total Minutes

Total Steps

THINGS TO GET DONE TODAY

MEAL TRACKER

Breakfast

Lunch

Dinner

Snack

REMINDER

TODAY I'M GRATEFUL FOR

NOTES

MONEY TRACKER

Money In	Money Out

DAILY PLANNER

DATE

S M T W T F S

TODAY'S GOALS

TODAY APPOINTMENT

Time	Event

SLEEP

MOOD

WATER INTAKE

Total :

EXERCISE

Total Minutes

Total Steps

THINGS TO GET DONE TODAY

MEAL TRACKER

Breakfast

Lunch

Dinner

Snack

REMINDER

TODAY I'M GRATEFUL FOR

NOTES

MONEY TRACKER

Money In	Money Out

DAILY PLANNER

DATE S M T W T F S

TODAY'S GOALS

TODAY APPOINTMENT

Time	Event

SLEEP

MOOD

WATER INTAKE

Total :

EXERCISE

Total Minutes

Total Steps

MEAL TRACKER

Breakfast

Lunch

Dinner

Snack

THINGS TO GET DONE TODAY

REMINDER

TODAY I'M GRATEFUL FOR

NOTES

MONEY TRACKER

Money In	Money Out

DAILY PLANNER

DATE

S M T W T F S

TODAY'S GOALS

TODAY APPOINTMENT

Time	Event

SLEEP

MOOD

WATER INTAKE

Total :

EXERCISE

Total Minutes

Total Steps

MEAL TRACKER

Breakfast

Lunch

Dinner

Snack

THINGS TO GET DONE TODAY

REMINDER

TODAY I'M GRATEFUL FOR

NOTES

MONEY TRACKER

Money In

Money Out

DAILY PLANNER

DATE S M T W T F S

TODAY'S GOALS

TODAY APPOINTMENT

Time	Event

SLEEP

MOOD

WATER INTAKE

Total :

EXERCISE

Total Minutes

Total Steps

MEAL TRACKER

Breakfast

Lunch

Dinner

Snack

THINGS TO GET DONE TODAY

REMINDER

MONEY TRACKER

Money In

Money Out

TODAY I'M GRATEFUL FOR

NOTES

DAILY PLANNER

DATE

S M T W T F S

TODAY'S GOALS

TODAY APPOINTMENT

Time	Event

SLEEP

MOOD

WATER INTAKE

Total :

THINGS TO GET DONE TODAY

EXERCISE

Total Minutes

Total Steps

MEAL TRACKER

Breakfast

Lunch

Dinner

Snack

REMINDER

TODAY I'M GRATEFUL FOR

NOTES

MONEY TRACKER

Money In	Money Out

DAILY PLANNER

DATE S M T W T F S

TODAY'S GOALS

TODAY APPOINTMENT

Time	Event

SLEEP

MOOD

WATER INTAKE

Total :

EXERCISE

Total Minutes

Total Steps

THINGS TO GET DONE TODAY

MEAL TRACKER

Breakfast

Lunch

Dinner

Snack

REMINDER

TODAY I'M GRATEFUL FOR

NOTES

MONEY TRACKER

Money In	Money Out

DAILY PLANNER

DATE

S M T W T F S

TODAY'S GOALS

TODAY APPOINTMENT

Time	Event

SLEEP

MOOD

WATER INTAKE

Total :

EXERCISE

Total Minutes

Total Steps

MEAL TRACKER

Breakfast

Lunch

Dinner

Snack

THINGS TO GET DONE TODAY

REMINDER

MONEY TRACKER

Money In

Money Out

TODAY I'M GRATEFUL FOR

NOTES

DAILY PLANNER

DATE S M T W T F S

TODAY'S GOALS

TODAY APPOINTMENT

Time	Event

SLEEP

MOOD

WATER INTAKE

Total :

EXERCISE

Total Minutes

Total Steps

THINGS TO GET DONE TODAY

MEAL TRACKER

Breakfast

Lunch

Dinner

Snack

REMINDER

TODAY I'M GRATEFUL FOR

NOTES

MONEY TRACKER

Money In	Money Out

NOTES

NOTES

OCTOBER

Monday	Tuesday	Wednesday	Thursday

To-Do

Affirmations For The month

Important Dates

Habits

To start	To stop

What do I love about myself?

Friday	Saturday	Sunday

Self-Care Activities

Main Goals

Appointments

Notes

OCTOBER BUDGET

Source Of Income	Amount
	$
	$
	$
Total Income	$

Expenses

Date	Bills	Budget	Actual
		$	$
		$	$
		$	$
		$	$
		$	$
		$	$
		$	$
		$	$
		$	$
		$	$
Total		$	$

Date	Groceries	Budget	Actual
		$	$
		$	$
		$	$
		$	$
		$	$
		$	$
		$	$
Total		$	$

Date	Transportation	Budget	Actual
		$	$
		$	$
		$	$
Total		$	$

Date	Shopping	Budget	Actual
		$	$
		$	$
		$	$
		$	$
		$	$
		$	$
Total		$	$

Date	Entertainment	Budget	Actual
		$	$
		$	$
		$	$
Total		$	$

Date	Fees & Charges	Budget	Actual
		$	$
		$	$
		$	$
Total		$	$

Date	Saving	Goal	Needed
		$	$
		$	$
		$	$
Total		$	$

TIME TRACKER

Use a green marker to highlight the hours you are focused and working on your goals. Over the course of the month – revisit and see what your productivity looks like.

DATE	AM	PM
1	1 2 3 4 5 6 7 8 9 10 11 12	1 2 3 4 5 6 7 8 9 10 11 12
2	1 2 3 4 5 6 7 8 9 10 11 12	1 2 3 4 5 6 7 8 9 10 11 12
3	1 2 3 4 5 6 7 8 9 10 11 12	1 2 3 4 5 6 7 8 9 10 11 12
4	1 2 3 4 5 6 7 8 9 10 11 12	1 2 3 4 5 6 7 8 9 10 11 12
5	1 2 3 4 5 6 7 8 9 10 11 12	1 2 3 4 5 6 7 8 9 10 11 12
6	1 2 3 4 5 6 7 8 9 10 11 12	1 2 3 4 5 6 7 8 9 10 11 12
7	1 2 3 4 5 6 7 8 9 10 11 12	1 2 3 4 5 6 7 8 9 10 11 12
8	1 2 3 4 5 6 7 8 9 10 11 12	1 2 3 4 5 6 7 8 9 10 11 12
9	1 2 3 4 5 6 7 8 9 10 11 12	1 2 3 4 5 6 7 8 9 10 11 12
10	1 2 3 4 5 6 7 8 9 10 11 12	1 2 3 4 5 6 7 8 9 10 11 12
11	1 2 3 4 5 6 7 8 9 10 11 12	1 2 3 4 5 6 7 8 9 10 11 12
12	1 2 3 4 5 6 7 8 9 10 11 12	1 2 3 4 5 6 7 8 9 10 11 12
13	1 2 3 4 5 6 7 8 9 10 11 12	1 2 3 4 5 6 7 8 9 10 11 12
14	1 2 3 4 5 6 7 8 9 10 11 12	1 2 3 4 5 6 7 8 9 10 11 12
15	1 2 3 4 5 6 7 8 9 10 11 12	1 2 3 4 5 6 7 8 9 10 11 12
16	1 2 3 4 5 6 7 8 9 10 11 12	1 2 3 4 5 6 7 8 9 10 11 12
17	1 2 3 4 5 6 7 8 9 10 11 12	1 2 3 4 5 6 7 8 9 10 11 12
18	1 2 3 4 5 6 7 8 9 10 11 12	1 2 3 4 5 6 7 8 9 10 11 12
19	1 2 3 4 5 6 7 8 9 10 11 12	1 2 3 4 5 6 7 8 9 10 11 12
20	1 2 3 4 5 6 7 8 9 10 11 12	1 2 3 4 5 6 7 8 9 10 11 12
21	1 2 3 4 5 6 7 8 9 10 11 12	1 2 3 4 5 6 7 8 9 10 11 12
22	1 2 3 4 5 6 7 8 9 10 11 12	1 2 3 4 5 6 7 8 9 10 11 12
23	1 2 3 4 5 6 7 8 9 10 11 12	1 2 3 4 5 6 7 8 9 10 11 12
24	1 2 3 4 5 6 7 8 9 10 11 12	1 2 3 4 5 6 7 8 9 10 11 12
25	1 2 3 4 5 6 7 8 9 10 11 12	1 2 3 4 5 6 7 8 9 10 11 12
26	1 2 3 4 5 6 7 8 9 10 11 12	1 2 3 4 5 6 7 8 9 10 11 12
27	1 2 3 4 5 6 7 8 9 10 11 12	1 2 3 4 5 6 7 8 9 10 11 12
28	1 2 3 4 5 6 7 8 9 10 11 12	1 2 3 4 5 6 7 8 9 10 11 12
29	1 2 3 4 5 6 7 8 9 10 11 12	1 2 3 4 5 6 7 8 9 10 11 12
30	1 2 3 4 5 6 7 8 9 10 11 12	1 2 3 4 5 6 7 8 9 10 11 12
31	1 2 3 4 5 6 7 8 9 10 11 12	1 2 3 4 5 6 7 8 9 10 11 12

CLIENT INFORMATION

Name
Phone
Email
Website
Address
Billing Adress
City
State Zip
D.O.B
Business Hours

Additional Information

Name
Phone
Email
Website
Address
Billing Adress
City
State Zip
D.O.B
Business Hours

Additional Information

Name
Phone
Email
Website
Address
Billing Adress
City
State Zip
D.O.B
Business Hours

Additional Information

Name
Phone
Email
Website
Address
Billing Adress
City
State Zip
D.O.B
Business Hours

Additional Information

CLIENT INFORMATION

Name
Phone
Email
Website
Address
Billing Adress
City
State Zip
D.O.B
Business Hours

Additional Information

Name
Phone
Email
Website
Address
Billing Adress
City
State Zip
D.O.B
Business Hours

Additional Information

Name
Phone
Email
Website
Address
Billing Adress
City
State Zip
D.O.B
Business Hours

Additional Information

Name
Phone
Email
Website
Address
Billing Adress
City
State Zip
D.O.B
Business Hours

Additional Information

MEETING NOTES

SUBJECT	DATE	TIME

AGENDA

ATTENDEES

-
-
-
-
-

IMPORTANT NOTES

SUBJECT	DATE	TIME

AGENDA

ATTENDEES

-
-
-
-
-

IMPORTANT NOTES

MEETING NOTES

SUBJECT

DATE

TIME

AGENDA

ATTENDEES

IMPORTANT NOTES

SUBJECT

DATE

TIME

AGENDA

ATTENDEES

IMPORTANT NOTES

OCTOBER SELF-CARE

Write a self-care activity and tick off each time you do self-care act.

ACTIVITIES	CHECKLIST
	1 2 3 4 5 6 7 8 9 10 11 12 13 14 15 16 17 18 19 20 21 22 23 24 25 26 27 28 29 30 31
	1 2 3 4 5 6 7 8 9 10 11 12 13 14 15 16 17 18 19 20 21 22 23 24 25 26 27 28 29 30 31
	1 2 3 4 5 6 7 8 9 10 11 12 13 14 15 16 17 18 19 20 21 22 23 24 25 26 27 28 29 30 31
	1 2 3 4 5 6 7 8 9 10 11 12 13 14 15 16 17 18 19 20 21 22 23 24 25 26 27 28 29 30 31
	1 2 3 4 5 6 7 8 9 10 11 12 13 14 15 16 17 18 19 20 21 22 23 24 25 26 27 28 29 30 31
	1 2 3 4 5 6 7 8 9 10 11 12 13 14 15 16 17 18 19 20 21 22 23 24 25 26 27 28 29 30 31
	1 2 3 4 5 6 7 8 9 10 11 12 13 14 15 16 17 18 19 20 21 22 23 24 25 26 27 28 29 30 31
	1 2 3 4 5 6 7 8 9 10 11 12 13 14 15 16 17 18 19 20 21 22 23 24 25 26 27 28 29 30 31
	1 2 3 4 5 6 7 8 9 10 11 12 13 14 15 16 17 18 19 20 21 22 23 24 25 26 27 28 29 30 31
	1 2 3 4 5 6 7 8 9 10 11 12 13 14 15 16 17 18 19 20 21 22 23 24 25 26 27 28 29 30 31

REFLECTION

HOW WILL YOU RATE THIS MONTH? ☆ ☆ ☆ ☆ ☆ ☆ ☆ ☆ ☆ ☆

MONTHLY WINS

-
-
-
-

HOW DOES IT MAKE ME FEEL?

-
-
-
-

CHALLENGES

-
-
-
-

HOW CAN I IMPROVE IT?

-
-
-
-

ACCOMPLISHED GOALS

UNACCOMPLISHED GOALS

GOALS NEXT MONTH

HABITS RETAINED

HABITS ELIMINATED

NEW HABITS DEVELOPED

THREE THINGS THAT I AM MOST GRATEFUL FOR THIS MONTH

1

2

3

TWO LIFE LESSONS I LEARNED THIS MONTH

1

2

ONE WORD THAT BEST DESCRIBES THIS MONTH

WEEKLY PLANNER

WEEK OF	
MOTIVATION	

MON	
TUE	
WED	
THUR	
FRI	
SAT	
SUN	

TO-DO

TOP PRIORITIES

NOTES

DAILY PLANNER

DATE S M T W T F S

TODAY'S GOALS

TODAY APPOINTMENT

Time	Event

SLEEP

MOOD

WATER INTAKE

Total :

EXERCISE

Total Minutes

Total Steps

MEAL TRACKER

Breakfast

Lunch

Dinner

Snack

THINGS TO GET DONE TODAY

REMINDER

TODAY I'M GRATEFUL FOR

NOTES

MONEY TRACKER

Money In	Money Out

DAILY PLANNER

DATE

S M T W T F S

TODAY'S GOALS

TODAY APPOINTMENT

Time	Event

SLEEP

MOOD

WATER INTAKE

Total :

EXERCISE

Total Minutes

Total Steps

THINGS TO GET DONE TODAY

MEAL TRACKER

Breakfast

Lunch

Dinner

Snack

REMINDER

TODAY I'M GRATEFUL FOR

NOTES

MONEY TRACKER

Money In	Money Out

DAILY PLANNER

DATE S M T W T F S

TODAY'S GOALS

TODAY APPOINTMENT

Time	Event

SLEEP

MOOD

WATER INTAKE

Total :

EXERCISE

Total Minutes

Total Steps

THINGS TO GET DONE TODAY

MEAL TRACKER

Breakfast

Lunch

Dinner

Snack

REMINDER

MONEY TRACKER

Money In

Money Out

TODAY I'M GRATEFUL FOR

NOTES

DAILY PLANNER

DATE

S M T W T F S

TODAY'S GOALS

TODAY APPOINTMENT

Time	Event

SLEEP

MOOD

WATER INTAKE

Total :

EXERCISE

Total Minutes

Total Steps

THINGS TO GET DONE TODAY

MEAL TRACKER

Breakfast

Lunch

Dinner

Snack

REMINDER

TODAY I'M GRATEFUL FOR

NOTES

MONEY TRACKER

Money In	Money Out

DAILY PLANNER

DATE

S M T W T F S

TODAY'S GOALS

TODAY APPOINTMENT

Time	Event

SLEEP

MOOD

WATER INTAKE

Total :

EXERCISE

Total Minutes

Total Steps

MEAL TRACKER

Breakfast

Lunch

Dinner

Snack

THINGS TO GET DONE TODAY

REMINDER

TODAY I'M GRATEFUL FOR

NOTES

MONEY TRACKER

Money In	Money Out

DAILY PLANNER

DATE

S M T W T F S

TODAY'S GOALS

TODAY APPOINTMENT

Time	Event

SLEEP

MOOD

WATER INTAKE

Total :

EXERCISE

Total Minutes

Total Steps

THINGS TO GET DONE TODAY

MEAL TRACKER

Breakfast

Lunch

Dinner

Snack

REMINDER

TODAY I'M GRATEFUL FOR

NOTES

MONEY TRACKER

Money In	Money Out

DAILY PLANNER

DATE S M T W T F S

TODAY'S GOALS

TODAY APPOINTMENT

Time	Event

SLEEP

MOOD

WATER INTAKE

Total :

EXERCISE

Total Minutes

Total Steps

MEAL TRACKER

Breakfast

Lunch

Dinner

Snack

THINGS TO GET DONE TODAY

REMINDER

TODAY I'M GRATEFUL FOR

NOTES

MONEY TRACKER

Money In	Money Out

WEEKLY PLANNER

WEEK OF

MOTIVATION

MON

TUE

WED

THUR

FRI

SAT

SUN

TO-DO

TOP PRIORITIES

NOTES

DAILY PLANNER

DATE S M T W T F S

TODAY'S GOALS

TODAY APPOINTMENT

Time	Event

SLEEP

MOOD

WATER INTAKE

Total :

EXERCISE

Total Minutes

Total Steps

THINGS TO GET DONE TODAY

MEAL TRACKER

Breakfast

Lunch

Dinner

Snack

REMINDER

TODAY I'M GRATEFUL FOR

NOTES

MONEY TRACKER

Money In	Money Out

DAILY PLANNER

DATE

S M T W T F S

TODAY'S GOALS

WATER INTAKE

Total :

MEAL TRACKER

Breakfast

Lunch

Dinner

Snack

MONEY TRACKER

Money In	Money Out

TODAY APPOINTMENT

Time	Event

THINGS TO GET DONE TODAY

TODAY I'M GRATEFUL FOR

SLEEP

MOOD

EXERCISE

Total Minutes

Total Steps

REMINDER

NOTES

DAILY PLANNER

DATE S M T W T F S

TODAY'S GOALS

TODAY APPOINTMENT

Time	Event

SLEEP

MOOD

WATER INTAKE

Total :

EXERCISE

Total Minutes

Total Steps

THINGS TO GET DONE TODAY

MEAL TRACKER

Breakfast

Lunch

Dinner

Snack

REMINDER

TODAY I'M GRATEFUL FOR

NOTES

MONEY TRACKER

Money In	Money Out

DAILY PLANNER

DATE

S M T W T F S

TODAY'S GOALS

TODAY APPOINTMENT

Time	Event

SLEEP

MOOD

WATER INTAKE

Total :

EXERCISE

Total Minutes

Total Steps

MEAL TRACKER

Breakfast

Lunch

Dinner

Snack

THINGS TO GET DONE TODAY

REMINDER

MONEY TRACKER

Money In

Money Out

TODAY I'M GRATEFUL FOR

NOTES

DAILY PLANNER

DATE S M T W T F S

TODAY'S GOALS

TODAY APPOINTMENT

Time	Event

SLEEP

MOOD

WATER INTAKE

Total :

EXERCISE

Total Minutes

Total Steps

THINGS TO GET DONE TODAY

MEAL TRACKER

Breakfast

Lunch

Dinner

Snack

REMINDER

TODAY I'M GRATEFUL FOR

NOTES

MONEY TRACKER

Money In	Money Out

DAILY PLANNER

DATE

S M T W T F S

TODAY'S GOALS

TODAY APPOINTMENT

Time	Event

SLEEP

MOOD

WATER INTAKE

Total :

EXERCISE

Total Minutes

Total Steps

THINGS TO GET DONE TODAY

MEAL TRACKER

Breakfast

Lunch

Dinner

Snack

REMINDER

MONEY TRACKER

Money In	Money Out

TODAY I'M GRATEFUL FOR

NOTES

DAILY PLANNER

DATE S M T W T F S

TODAY'S GOALS

TODAY APPOINTMENT

Time	Event

SLEEP

MOOD

WATER INTAKE

Total :

EXERCISE

Total Minutes

Total Steps

MEAL TRACKER

Breakfast

Lunch

Dinner

Snack

THINGS TO GET DONE TODAY

REMINDER

MONEY TRACKER

Money In

Money Out

TODAY I'M GRATEFUL FOR

NOTES

WEEKLY PLANNER

WEEK OF	
MOTIVATION	

MON

TUE

WED

THUR

FRI

SAT

SUN

TO-DO

TOP PRIORITIES

NOTES

DAILY PLANNER

DATE S M T W T F S

TODAY'S GOALS

TODAY APPOINTMENT

Time	Event

SLEEP

MOOD

WATER INTAKE

Total :

EXERCISE

Total Minutes

Total Steps

THINGS TO GET DONE TODAY

MEAL TRACKER

Breakfast

Lunch

Dinner

Snack

REMINDER

TODAY I'M GRATEFUL FOR

NOTES

MONEY TRACKER

Money In	Money Out

DAILY PLANNER

DATE

S M T W T F S

TODAY'S GOALS

TODAY APPOINTMENT

Time	Event

SLEEP

MOOD

WATER INTAKE

Total :

EXERCISE

Total Minutes

Total Steps

MEAL TRACKER

Breakfast

Lunch

Dinner

Snack

THINGS TO GET DONE TODAY

REMINDER

MONEY TRACKER

Money In	Money Out

TODAY I'M GRATEFUL FOR

NOTES

DAILY PLANNER

DATE S M T W T F S

TODAY'S GOALS

TODAY APPOINTMENT

Time	Event

SLEEP

MOOD

WATER INTAKE

Total :

EXERCISE

Total Minutes

Total Steps

MEAL TRACKER

Breakfast

Lunch

Dinner

Snack

THINGS TO GET DONE TODAY

REMINDER

MONEY TRACKER

Money In

Money Out

TODAY I'M GRATEFUL FOR

NOTES

DAILY PLANNER

DATE

S M T W T F S

TODAY'S GOALS

TODAY APPOINTMENT

Time	Event

SLEEP

MOOD

WATER INTAKE

Total :

EXERCISE

Total Minutes

Total Steps

MEAL TRACKER

Breakfast

Lunch

Dinner

Snack

THINGS TO GET DONE TODAY

REMINDER

TODAY I'M GRATEFUL FOR

NOTES

MONEY TRACKER

Money In	Money Out

DAILY PLANNER

DATE S M T W T F S

TODAY'S GOALS

TODAY APPOINTMENT

Time	Event

SLEEP

MOOD

WATER INTAKE

Total :

EXERCISE

Total Minutes

Total Steps

MEAL TRACKER

Breakfast

Lunch

Dinner

Snack

THINGS TO GET DONE TODAY

REMINDER

MONEY TRACKER

Money In	Money Out

TODAY I'M GRATEFUL FOR

NOTES

DAILY PLANNER

DATE

S M T W T F S

TODAY'S GOALS

TODAY APPOINTMENT

Time	Event

SLEEP

MOOD

WATER INTAKE

Total :

EXERCISE

Total Minutes

Total Steps

THINGS TO GET DONE TODAY

MEAL TRACKER

Breakfast

Lunch

Dinner

Snack

REMINDER

TODAY I'M GRATEFUL FOR

NOTES

MONEY TRACKER

Money In	Money Out

DAILY PLANNER

DATE S M T W T F S

TODAY'S GOALS

TODAY APPOINTMENT

Time	Event

SLEEP

MOOD

WATER INTAKE

Total :

EXERCISE

Total Minutes

Total Steps

MEAL TRACKER

Breakfast

Lunch

Dinner

Snack

THINGS TO GET DONE TODAY

REMINDER

MONEY TRACKER

Money In

Money Out

TODAY I'M GRATEFUL FOR

NOTES

WEEKLY PLANNER

WEEK OF

MOTIVATION

MON

TUE

WED

THUR

FRI

SAT

SUN

TO-DO

TOP PRIORITIES

NOTES

DAILY PLANNER

DATE S M T W T F S

TODAY'S GOALS

TODAY APPOINTMENT

Time	Event

SLEEP

MOOD

WATER INTAKE

Total :

EXERCISE

Total Minutes

Total Steps

MEAL TRACKER

Breakfast

Lunch

Dinner

Snack

THINGS TO GET DONE TODAY

REMINDER

TODAY I'M GRATEFUL FOR

NOTES

MONEY TRACKER

Money In	Money Out

DAILY PLANNER

DATE

S M T W T F S

TODAY'S GOALS

TODAY APPOINTMENT

Time	Event

SLEEP

MOOD

WATER INTAKE

Total :

EXERCISE

Total Minutes

Total Steps

THINGS TO GET DONE TODAY

MEAL TRACKER

Breakfast

Lunch

Dinner

Snack

REMINDER

TODAY I'M GRATEFUL FOR

NOTES

MONEY TRACKER

Money In	Money Out

DAILY PLANNER

DATE S M T W T F S

TODAY'S GOALS

TODAY APPOINTMENT

Time	Event

SLEEP

MOOD

WATER INTAKE

Total :

EXERCISE

Total Minutes

Total Steps

THINGS TO GET DONE TODAY

MEAL TRACKER

Breakfast

Lunch

Dinner

Snack

REMINDER

TODAY I'M GRATEFUL FOR

NOTES

MONEY TRACKER

Money In	Money Out

DAILY PLANNER

DATE

S M T W T F S

TODAY'S GOALS

TODAY APPOINTMENT

Time	Event

SLEEP

MOOD

WATER INTAKE

Total :

EXERCISE

Total Minutes

Total Steps

MEAL TRACKER

Breakfast

Lunch

Dinner

Snack

THINGS TO GET DONE TODAY

REMINDER

TODAY I'M GRATEFUL FOR

NOTES

MONEY TRACKER

Money In	Money Out

DAILY PLANNER

DATE S M T W T F S

TODAY'S GOALS

TODAY APPOINTMENT

Time	Event

SLEEP

MOOD

WATER INTAKE

Total :

EXERCISE

Total Minutes

Total Steps

MEAL TRACKER

Breakfast

Lunch

Dinner

Snack

THINGS TO GET DONE TODAY

REMINDER

TODAY I'M GRATEFUL FOR

NOTES

MONEY TRACKER

Money In	Money Out

DAILY PLANNER

DATE

S M T W T F S

TODAY'S GOALS

TODAY APPOINTMENT

Time	Event

SLEEP

MOOD

WATER INTAKE

Total :

EXERCISE

Total Minutes

Total Steps

THINGS TO GET DONE TODAY

MEAL TRACKER

Breakfast

Lunch

Dinner

Snack

REMINDER

TODAY I'M GRATEFUL FOR

NOTES

MONEY TRACKER

Money In	Money Out

DAILY PLANNER

DATE S M T W T F S

TODAY'S GOALS

TODAY APPOINTMENT

Time	Event

SLEEP

MOOD

WATER INTAKE

Total :

EXERCISE

Total Minutes

Total Steps

MEAL TRACKER

Breakfast

Lunch

Dinner

Snack

THINGS TO GET DONE TODAY

REMINDER

MONEY TRACKER

Money In	Money Out

TODAY I'M GRATEFUL FOR

NOTES

DAILY PLANNER

DATE

S M T W T F S

TODAY'S GOALS

TODAY APPOINTMENT

Time	Event

SLEEP

MOOD

WATER INTAKE

Total :

EXERCISE

Total Minutes

Total Steps

MEAL TRACKER

Breakfast

Lunch

Dinner

Snack

THINGS TO GET DONE TODAY

REMINDER

MONEY TRACKER

Money In	Money Out

TODAY I'M GRATEFUL FOR

NOTES

DAILY PLANNER

DATE S M T W T F S

TODAY'S GOALS

TODAY APPOINTMENT

Time	Event

SLEEP

MOOD

WATER INTAKE

Total :

EXERCISE

Total Minutes

Total Steps

MEAL TRACKER

Breakfast

Lunch

Dinner

Snack

THINGS TO GET DONE TODAY

REMINDER

TODAY I'M GRATEFUL FOR

NOTES

MONEY TRACKER

Money In	Money Out

DAILY PLANNER

DATE

S M T W T F S

TODAY'S GOALS

TODAY APPOINTMENT

Time	Event

SLEEP

MOOD

WATER INTAKE

Total :

EXERCISE

Total Minutes

Total Steps

MEAL TRACKER

Breakfast

Lunch

Dinner

Snack

THINGS TO GET DONE TODAY

REMINDER

MONEY TRACKER

Money In	Money Out

TODAY I'M GRATEFUL FOR

NOTES

NOTES

NOVEMBER

Monday	Tuesday	Wednesday	Thursday

To-Do

Affirmations For The month

Important Dates

Habits

To start	To stop

What do I love about myself?

Friday | Saturday | Sunday

Self-Care Activities

Main Goals

Appointments

Notes

NOVEMBER BUDGET

Source Of Income	Amount
	$
	$
	$
Total Income	$

Expenses

Date	Bills	Budget	Actual
		$	$
		$	$
		$	$
		$	$
		$	$
		$	$
		$	$
		$	$
		$	$
		$	$
Total		$	$

Date	Groceries	Budget	Actual
		$	$
		$	$
		$	$
		$	$
		$	$
		$	$
		$	$
Total		$	$

Date	Transportation	Budget	Actual
		$	$
		$	$
		$	$
Total		$	$

Date	Shopping	Budget	Actual
		$	$
		$	$
		$	$
		$	$
		$	$
		$	$
Total		$	$

Date	Entertainment	Budget	Actual
		$	$
		$	$
		$	$
Total		$	$

Date	Fees & Charges	Budget	Actual
		$	$
		$	$
		$	$
Total		$	$

Date	Saving	Goal	Needed
		$	$
		$	$
		$	$
Total		$	$

TIME TRACKER

Use a green marker to highlight the hours you are focused and working on your goals. Over the course of the month – revisit and see what your productivity looks like.

DATE	AM												PM											
1	1	2	3	4	5	6	7	8	9	10	11	12	1	2	3	4	5	6	7	8	9	10	11	12
2	1	2	3	4	5	6	7	8	9	10	11	12	1	2	3	4	5	6	7	8	9	10	11	12
3	1	2	3	4	5	6	7	8	9	10	11	12	1	2	3	4	5	6	7	8	9	10	11	12
4	1	2	3	4	5	6	7	8	9	10	11	12	1	2	3	4	5	6	7	8	9	10	11	12
5	1	2	3	4	5	6	7	8	9	10	11	12	1	2	3	4	5	6	7	8	9	10	11	12
6	1	2	3	4	5	6	7	8	9	10	11	12	1	2	3	4	5	6	7	8	9	10	11	12
7	1	2	3	4	5	6	7	8	9	10	11	12	1	2	3	4	5	6	7	8	9	10	11	12
8	1	2	3	4	5	6	7	8	9	10	11	12	1	2	3	4	5	6	7	8	9	10	11	12
9	1	2	3	4	5	6	7	8	9	10	11	12	1	2	3	4	5	6	7	8	9	10	11	12
10	1	2	3	4	5	6	7	8	9	10	11	12	1	2	3	4	5	6	7	8	9	10	11	12
11	1	2	3	4	5	6	7	8	9	10	11	12	1	2	3	4	5	6	7	8	9	10	11	12
12	1	2	3	4	5	6	7	8	9	10	11	12	1	2	3	4	5	6	7	8	9	10	11	12
13	1	2	3	4	5	6	7	8	9	10	11	12	1	2	3	4	5	6	7	8	9	10	11	12
14	1	2	3	4	5	6	7	8	9	10	11	12	1	2	3	4	5	6	7	8	9	10	11	12
15	1	2	3	4	5	6	7	8	9	10	11	12	1	2	3	4	5	6	7	8	9	10	11	12
16	1	2	3	4	5	6	7	8	9	10	11	12	1	2	3	4	5	6	7	8	9	10	11	12
17	1	2	3	4	5	6	7	8	9	10	11	12	1	2	3	4	5	6	7	8	9	10	11	12
18	1	2	3	4	5	6	7	8	9	10	11	12	1	2	3	4	5	6	7	8	9	10	11	12
19	1	2	3	4	5	6	7	8	9	10	11	12	1	2	3	4	5	6	7	8	9	10	11	12
20	1	2	3	4	5	6	7	8	9	10	11	12	1	2	3	4	5	6	7	8	9	10	11	12
21	1	2	3	4	5	6	7	8	9	10	11	12	1	2	3	4	5	6	7	8	9	10	11	12
22	1	2	3	4	5	6	7	8	9	10	11	12	1	2	3	4	5	6	7	8	9	10	11	12
23	1	2	3	4	5	6	7	8	9	10	11	12	1	2	3	4	5	6	7	8	9	10	11	12
24	1	2	3	4	5	6	7	8	9	10	11	12	1	2	3	4	5	6	7	8	9	10	11	12
25	1	2	3	4	5	6	7	8	9	10	11	12	1	2	3	4	5	6	7	8	9	10	11	12
26	1	2	3	4	5	6	7	8	9	10	11	12	1	2	3	4	5	6	7	8	9	10	11	12
27	1	2	3	4	5	6	7	8	9	10	11	12	1	2	3	4	5	6	7	8	9	10	11	12
28	1	2	3	4	5	6	7	8	9	10	11	12	1	2	3	4	5	6	7	8	9	10	11	12
29	1	2	3	4	5	6	7	8	9	10	11	12	1	2	3	4	5	6	7	8	9	10	11	12
30	1	2	3	4	5	6	7	8	9	10	11	12	1	2	3	4	5	6	7	8	9	10	11	12
31	1	2	3	4	5	6	7	8	9	10	11	12	1	2	3	4	5	6	7	8	9	10	11	12

CLIENT INFORMATION

Name
Phone
Email
Website
Address
Billing Adress
City
State Zip
D.O.B
Business Hours

Additional Information

Name
Phone
Email
Website
Address
Billing Adress
City
State Zip
D.O.B
Business Hours

Additional Information

Name
Phone
Email
Website
Address
Billing Adress
City
State Zip
D.O.B
Business Hours

Additional Information

Name
Phone
Email
Website
Address
Billing Adress
City
State Zip
D.O.B
Business Hours

Additional Information

CLIENT INFORMATION

Name
Phone
Email
Website
Address
Billing Adress
City
State Zip
D.O.B
Business Hours

Additional Information

Name
Phone
Email
Website
Address
Billing Adress
City
State Zip
D.O.B
Business Hours

Additional Information

Name
Phone
Email
Website
Address
Billing Adress
City
State Zip
D.O.B
Business Hours

Additional Information

Name
Phone
Email
Website
Address
Billing Adress
City
State Zip
D.O.B
Business Hours

Additional Information

MEETING NOTES

SUBJECT	DATE	TIME

AGENDA

ATTENDEES

IMPORTANT NOTES

SUBJECT	DATE	TIME

AGENDA

ATTENDEES

IMPORTANT NOTES

MEETING NOTES

SUBJECT	DATE	TIME

AGENDA

ATTENDEES	IMPORTANT NOTES
• • • • •	

SUBJECT	DATE	TIME

AGENDA

ATTENDEES	IMPORTANT NOTES
• • • • •	

NOVEMBER SELF-CARE

Write a self-care activity and tick off each time you do self-care act.

ACTIVITIES	CHECKLIST
	1 2 3 4 5 6 7 8 9 10 11 12 13 14 15 16 17 18 19 20 21 22 23 24 25 26 27 28 29 30 31
	1 2 3 4 5 6 7 8 9 10 11 12 13 14 15 16 17 18 19 20 21 22 23 24 25 26 27 28 29 30 31
	1 2 3 4 5 6 7 8 9 10 11 12 13 14 15 16 17 18 19 20 21 22 23 24 25 26 27 28 29 30 31
	1 2 3 4 5 6 7 8 9 10 11 12 13 14 15 16 17 18 19 20 21 22 23 24 25 26 27 28 29 30 31
	1 2 3 4 5 6 7 8 9 10 11 12 13 14 15 16 17 18 19 20 21 22 23 24 25 26 27 28 29 30 31
	1 2 3 4 5 6 7 8 9 10 11 12 13 14 15 16 17 18 19 20 21 22 23 24 25 26 27 28 29 30 31
	1 2 3 4 5 6 7 8 9 10 11 12 13 14 15 16 17 18 19 20 21 22 23 24 25 26 27 28 29 30 31
	1 2 3 4 5 6 7 8 9 10 11 12 13 14 15 16 17 18 19 20 21 22 23 24 25 26 27 28 29 30 31
	1 2 3 4 5 6 7 8 9 10 11 12 13 14 15 16 17 18 19 20 21 22 23 24 25 26 27 28 29 30 31
	1 2 3 4 5 6 7 8 9 10 11 12 13 14 15 16 17 18 19 20 21 22 23 24 25 26 27 28 29 30 31

REFLECTION

HOW WILL YOU RATE THIS MONTH? ☆ ☆ ☆ ☆ ☆ ☆ ☆ ☆ ☆ ☆

MONTHLY WINS	HOW DOES IT MAKE ME FEEL?
•	•
•	•
•	•
•	•

CHALLENGES	HOW CAN I IMPROVE IT?
•	•
•	•
•	•
•	•

ACCOMPLISHED GOALS	UNACCOMPLISHED GOALS	GOALS NEXT MONTH

HABITS RETAINED	HABITS ELIMINATED	NEW HABITS DEVELOPED

THREE THINGS THAT I AM MOST GRATEFUL FOR THIS MONTH

1	2	3

TWO LIFE LESSONS I LEARNED THIS MONTH

1	2

ONE WORD THAT BEST DESCRIBES THIS MONTH

WEEKLY PLANNER

WEEK OF

MOTIVATION

MON

TUE

WED

THUR

FRI

SAT

SUN

TO-DO

TOP PRIORITIES

NOTES

DAILY PLANNER

DATE S M T W T F S

TODAY'S GOALS

TODAY APPOINTMENT

Time	Event

SLEEP

MOOD

WATER INTAKE

Total :

EXERCISE

Total Minutes

Total Steps

MEAL TRACKER

Breakfast

Lunch

Dinner

Snack

THINGS TO GET DONE TODAY

REMINDER

MONEY TRACKER

Money In	Money Out

TODAY I'M GRATEFUL FOR

NOTES

DAILY PLANNER

DATE

S M T W T F S

TODAY'S GOALS

TODAY APPOINTMENT

Time	Event

SLEEP

MOOD

WATER INTAKE

Total :

EXERCISE

Total Minutes

Total Steps

MEAL TRACKER

Breakfast

Lunch

Dinner

Snack

THINGS TO GET DONE TODAY

REMINDER

MONEY TRACKER

Money In

Money Out

TODAY I'M GRATEFUL FOR

NOTES

DAILY PLANNER

DATE S M T W T F S

TODAY'S GOALS

TODAY APPOINTMENT

Time	Event

SLEEP

MOOD

WATER INTAKE

Total :

THINGS TO GET DONE TODAY

EXERCISE

Total Minutes

Total Steps

MEAL TRACKER

Breakfast

Lunch

Dinner

Snack

REMINDER

TODAY I'M GRATEFUL FOR

NOTES

MONEY TRACKER

Money In	Money Out

DAILY PLANNER

DATE

S M T W T F S

TODAY'S GOALS

TODAY APPOINTMENT

Time	Event

SLEEP

MOOD

WATER INTAKE

Total :

EXERCISE

Total Minutes

Total Steps

THINGS TO GET DONE TODAY

MEAL TRACKER

Breakfast

Lunch

Dinner

Snack

REMINDER

TODAY I'M GRATEFUL FOR

NOTES

MONEY TRACKER

Money In	Money Out

DAILY PLANNER

DATE

S M T W T F S

TODAY'S GOALS

TODAY APPOINTMENT

Time	Event

SLEEP

MOOD

WATER INTAKE

Total :

EXERCISE

Total Minutes

Total Steps

THINGS TO GET DONE TODAY

MEAL TRACKER

Breakfast

Lunch

Dinner

Snack

REMINDER

TODAY I'M GRATEFUL FOR

NOTES

MONEY TRACKER

Money In

Money Out

DAILY PLANNER

DATE

S M T W T F S

TODAY'S GOALS

TODAY APPOINTMENT

Time	Event

SLEEP

MOOD

WATER INTAKE

Total :

EXERCISE

Total Minutes

Total Steps

THINGS TO GET DONE TODAY

MEAL TRACKER

Breakfast

Lunch

Dinner

Snack

REMINDER

TODAY I'M GRATEFUL FOR

NOTES

MONEY TRACKER

Money In	Money Out

DAILY PLANNER

DATE S M T W T F S

TODAY'S GOALS

TODAY APPOINTMENT

Time	Event

SLEEP

MOOD

WATER INTAKE

Total :

EXERCISE

Total Minutes

Total Steps

THINGS TO GET DONE TODAY

MEAL TRACKER

Breakfast

Lunch

Dinner

Snack

REMINDER

TODAY I'M GRATEFUL FOR

NOTES

MONEY TRACKER

Money In

Money Out

WEEKLY PLANNER

WEEK OF

MOTIVATION

MON

TUE

WED

THUR

FRI

SAT

SUN

TO-DO

TOP PRIORITIES

NOTES

DAILY PLANNER

DATE S M T W T F S

TODAY'S GOALS

TODAY APPOINTMENT

Time	Event

SLEEP

MOOD

WATER INTAKE

Total :

EXERCISE

Total Minutes

Total Steps

MEAL TRACKER

Breakfast

Lunch

Dinner

Snack

THINGS TO GET DONE TODAY

REMINDER

TODAY I'M GRATEFUL FOR

NOTES

MONEY TRACKER

Money In	Money Out

DAILY PLANNER

DATE

S M T W T F S

TODAY'S GOALS

TODAY APPOINTMENT

Time	Event

SLEEP

MOOD

WATER INTAKE

Total :

EXERCISE

Total Minutes

Total Steps

MEAL TRACKER

Breakfast

Lunch

Dinner

Snack

THINGS TO GET DONE TODAY

REMINDER

TODAY I'M GRATEFUL FOR

NOTES

MONEY TRACKER

Money In	Money Out

DAILY PLANNER

DATE S M T W T F S

TODAY'S GOALS

TODAY APPOINTMENT

Time	Event

SLEEP

MOOD

WATER INTAKE

Total :

EXERCISE

Total Minutes

Total Steps

MEAL TRACKER

Breakfast

Lunch

Dinner

Snack

THINGS TO GET DONE TODAY

REMINDER

MONEY TRACKER

Money In	Money Out

TODAY I'M GRATEFUL FOR

NOTES

DAILY PLANNER

DATE

S M T W T F S

TODAY'S GOALS

TODAY APPOINTMENT

Time	Event

SLEEP

MOOD

WATER INTAKE

Total :

EXERCISE

Total Minutes

Total Steps

THINGS TO GET DONE TODAY

MEAL TRACKER

Breakfast

Lunch

Dinner

Snack

REMINDER

TODAY I'M GRATEFUL FOR

NOTES

MONEY TRACKER

Money In

Money Out

DAILY PLANNER

DATE S M T W T F S

TODAY'S GOALS

TODAY APPOINTMENT

Time	Event

SLEEP

MOOD

WATER INTAKE

Total :

EXERCISE

Total Minutes

Total Steps

MEAL TRACKER

Breakfast

Lunch

Dinner

Snack

THINGS TO GET DONE TODAY

REMINDER

MONEY TRACKER

Money In	Money Out

TODAY I'M GRATEFUL FOR

NOTES

DAILY PLANNER

DATE

S M T W T F S

TODAY'S GOALS

TODAY APPOINTMENT

Time	Event

SLEEP

MOOD

WATER INTAKE

Total :

EXERCISE

Total Minutes

Total Steps

MEAL TRACKER

Breakfast

Lunch

Dinner

Snack

THINGS TO GET DONE TODAY

REMINDER

TODAY I'M GRATEFUL FOR

MONEY TRACKER

Money In	Money Out

NOTES

DAILY PLANNER

DATE S M T W T F S

TODAY'S GOALS

TODAY APPOINTMENT

Time	Event

SLEEP

MOOD

WATER INTAKE

Total :

EXERCISE

Total Minutes

Total Steps

THINGS TO GET DONE TODAY

MEAL TRACKER

Breakfast

Lunch

Dinner

Snack

REMINDER

TODAY I'M GRATEFUL FOR

NOTES

MONEY TRACKER

Money In	Money Out

WEEKLY PLANNER

WEEK OF

MOTIVATION

MON

TUE

WED

THUR

FRI

SAT

SUN

TO-DO

TOP PRIORITIES

NOTES

DAILY PLANNER

DATE S M T W T F S

TODAY'S GOALS

TODAY APPOINTMENT

Time	Event

SLEEP

MOOD

WATER INTAKE

Total :

EXERCISE

Total Minutes

Total Steps

THINGS TO GET DONE TODAY

MEAL TRACKER

Breakfast

Lunch

Dinner

Snack

REMINDER

TODAY I'M GRATEFUL FOR

NOTES

MONEY TRACKER

Money In	Money Out

DAILY PLANNER

DATE

S M T W T F S

TODAY'S GOALS

TODAY APPOINTMENT

Time	Event

SLEEP

MOOD

WATER INTAKE

Total :

EXERCISE

Total Minutes

Total Steps

MEAL TRACKER

Breakfast

Lunch

Dinner

Snack

THINGS TO GET DONE TODAY

REMINDER

MONEY TRACKER

Money In	Money Out

TODAY I'M GRATEFUL FOR

NOTES

DAILY PLANNER

DATE S M T W T F S

TODAY'S GOALS

TODAY APPOINTMENT

Time	Event

SLEEP

MOOD

WATER INTAKE

Total :

EXERCISE

Total Minutes

Total Steps

THINGS TO GET DONE TODAY

MEAL TRACKER

Breakfast

Lunch

Dinner

Snack

REMINDER

TODAY I'M GRATEFUL FOR

NOTES

MONEY TRACKER

Money In	Money Out

DAILY PLANNER

DATE

S M T W T F S

TODAY'S GOALS

TODAY APPOINTMENT

Time	Event

SLEEP

MOOD

WATER INTAKE

Total :

EXERCISE

Total Minutes

Total Steps

MEAL TRACKER

Breakfast

Lunch

Dinner

Snack

THINGS TO GET DONE TODAY

REMINDER

MONEY TRACKER

Money In

Money Out

TODAY I'M GRATEFUL FOR

NOTES

DAILY PLANNER

DATE S M T W T F S

TODAY'S GOALS

TODAY APPOINTMENT

Time	Event

SLEEP

MOOD

WATER INTAKE

Total :

EXERCISE

Total Minutes

Total Steps

MEAL TRACKER

Breakfast

Lunch

Dinner

Snack

THINGS TO GET DONE TODAY

REMINDER

TODAY I'M GRATEFUL FOR

NOTES

MONEY TRACKER

Money In	Money Out

DAILY PLANNER

DATE

S M T W T F S

TODAY'S GOALS

TODAY APPOINTMENT

Time	Event

SLEEP

MOOD

WATER INTAKE

Total :

EXERCISE

Total Minutes

Total Steps

THINGS TO GET DONE TODAY

MEAL TRACKER

Breakfast

Lunch

Dinner

Snack

REMINDER

TODAY I'M GRATEFUL FOR

NOTES

MONEY TRACKER

Money In	Money Out

DAILY PLANNER

DATE S M T W T F S

TODAY'S GOALS

TODAY APPOINTMENT

Time	Event

SLEEP

MOOD

WATER INTAKE

Total :

EXERCISE

Total Minutes

Total Steps

THINGS TO GET DONE TODAY

MEAL TRACKER

Breakfast

Lunch

Dinner

Snack

REMINDER

TODAY I'M GRATEFUL FOR

MONEY TRACKER

Money In

Money Out

NOTES

WEEKLY PLANNER

WEEK OF

MOTIVATION

MON

TUE

WED

THUR

FRI

SAT

SUN

TO-DO

TOP PRIORITIES

NOTES

DAILY PLANNER

DATE S M T W T F S

TODAY'S GOALS

TODAY APPOINTMENT

Time	Event

SLEEP

MOOD

WATER INTAKE

Total :

EXERCISE

Total Minutes

Total Steps

THINGS TO GET DONE TODAY

MEAL TRACKER

Breakfast

Lunch

Dinner

Snack

REMINDER

TODAY I'M GRATEFUL FOR

NOTES

MONEY TRACKER

Money In	Money Out

DAILY PLANNER

DATE

S M T W T F S

TODAY'S GOALS

TODAY APPOINTMENT

Time	Event

SLEEP

MOOD

WATER INTAKE

Total :

EXERCISE

Total Minutes

Total Steps

THINGS TO GET DONE TODAY

MEAL TRACKER

Breakfast

Lunch

Dinner

Snack

REMINDER

TODAY I'M GRATEFUL FOR

NOTES

MONEY TRACKER

Money In	Money Out

DAILY PLANNER

DATE S M T W T F S

TODAY'S GOALS

TODAY APPOINTMENT

Time	Event

SLEEP

MOOD

WATER INTAKE

Total :

EXERCISE

Total Minutes

Total Steps

MEAL TRACKER

Breakfast

Lunch

Dinner

Snack

THINGS TO GET DONE TODAY

REMINDER

TODAY I'M GRATEFUL FOR

NOTES

MONEY TRACKER

Money In	Money Out

DAILY PLANNER

DATE

S M T W T F S

TODAY'S GOALS

TODAY APPOINTMENT

Time	Event

SLEEP

MOOD

WATER INTAKE

Total :

THINGS TO GET DONE TODAY

EXERCISE

Total Minutes

Total Steps

MEAL TRACKER

Breakfast

Lunch

Dinner

Snack

REMINDER

TODAY I'M GRATEFUL FOR

NOTES

MONEY TRACKER

Money In	Money Out

DAILY PLANNER

DATE S M T W T F S

TODAY'S GOALS

TODAY APPOINTMENT

Time	Event

SLEEP

MOOD

WATER INTAKE

Total :

EXERCISE

Total Minutes

Total Steps

MEAL TRACKER

Breakfast

Lunch

Dinner

Snack

THINGS TO GET DONE TODAY

REMINDER

MONEY TRACKER

Money In

Money Out

TODAY I'M GRATEFUL FOR

NOTES

DAILY PLANNER

DATE

S M T W T F S

TODAY'S GOALS

WATER INTAKE

Total :

MEAL TRACKER

Breakfast

Lunch

Dinner

Snack

MONEY TRACKER

Money In

Money Out

TODAY APPOINTMENT

Time	Event

THINGS TO GET DONE TODAY

TODAY I'M GRATEFUL FOR

SLEEP

MOOD

EXERCISE

Total Minutes

Total Steps

REMINDER

NOTES

DAILY PLANNER

DATE S M T W T F S

TODAY'S GOALS

TODAY APPOINTMENT

Time	Event

SLEEP

MOOD

WATER INTAKE

Total :

EXERCISE

Total Minutes

Total Steps

MEAL TRACKER

Breakfast

Lunch

Dinner

Snack

THINGS TO GET DONE TODAY

REMINDER

MONEY TRACKER

Money In	Money Out

TODAY I'M GRATEFUL FOR

NOTES

DAILY PLANNER

DATE

S M T W T F S

TODAY'S GOALS

TODAY APPOINTMENT

Time	Event

SLEEP

MOOD

WATER INTAKE

Total :

EXERCISE

Total Minutes

Total Steps

THINGS TO GET DONE TODAY

MEAL TRACKER

Breakfast

Lunch

Dinner

Snack

REMINDER

TODAY I'M GRATEFUL FOR

NOTES

MONEY TRACKER

Money In	Money Out

DAILY PLANNER

DATE S M T W T F S

TODAY'S GOALS

TODAY APPOINTMENT

Time	Event

SLEEP

MOOD

WATER INTAKE

Total :

MEAL TRACKER

Breakfast

Lunch

Dinner

Snack

MONEY TRACKER

Money In	Money Out

THINGS TO GET DONE TODAY

EXERCISE

Total Minutes

Total Steps

REMINDER

TODAY I'M GRATEFUL FOR

NOTES

NOTES

NOTES

DECEMBER

To-Do

- [ ]
- [ ]
- [ ]
- [ ]
- [ ]
- [ ]
- [ ]
- [ ]
- [ ]
- [ ]
- [ ]
- [ ]
- [ ]
- [ ]

Monday	Tuesday	Wednesday	Thursday

Affirmations For The month

Important Dates

Habits

To start	To stop

What do I love about myself?

Friday	Saturday	Sunday

Self-Care Activities

Main Goals

Appointments

Notes

DECEMBER BUDGET

Source Of Income	Amount
	$
	$
	$
Total Income	$

Expenses

Date	Bills	Budget	Actual
		$	$
		$	$
		$	$
		$	$
		$	$
		$	$
		$	$
		$	$
		$	$
		$	$
Total		$	$

Date	Groceries	Budget	Actual
		$	$
		$	$
		$	$
		$	$
		$	$
		$	$
		$	$
Total		$	$

Date	Transportation	Budget	Actual
		$	$
		$	$
		$	$
Total		$	$

Date	Shopping	Budget	Actual
		$	$
		$	$
		$	$
		$	$
		$	$
		$	$
Total		$	$

Date	Entertainment	Budget	Actual
		$	$
		$	$
		$	$
Total		$	$

Date	Fees & Charges	Budget	Actual
		$	$
		$	$
		$	$
Total		$	$

Date	Saving	Goal	Needed
		$	$
		$	$
		$	$
Total		$	$

TIME TRACKER

Use a green marker to highlight the hours you are focused and working on your goals. Over the course of the month – revisit and see what your productivity looks like.

DATE	AM												PM											
1	1	2	3	4	5	6	7	8	9	10	11	12	1	2	3	4	5	6	7	8	9	10	11	12
2	1	2	3	4	5	6	7	8	9	10	11	12	1	2	3	4	5	6	7	8	9	10	11	12
3	1	2	3	4	5	6	7	8	9	10	11	12	1	2	3	4	5	6	7	8	9	10	11	12
4	1	2	3	4	5	6	7	8	9	10	11	12	1	2	3	4	5	6	7	8	9	10	11	12
5	1	2	3	4	5	6	7	8	9	10	11	12	1	2	3	4	5	6	7	8	9	10	11	12
6	1	2	3	4	5	6	7	8	9	10	11	12	1	2	3	4	5	6	7	8	9	10	11	12
7	1	2	3	4	5	6	7	8	9	10	11	12	1	2	3	4	5	6	7	8	9	10	11	12
8	1	2	3	4	5	6	7	8	9	10	11	12	1	2	3	4	5	6	7	8	9	10	11	12
9	1	2	3	4	5	6	7	8	9	10	11	12	1	2	3	4	5	6	7	8	9	10	11	12
10	1	2	3	4	5	6	7	8	9	10	11	12	1	2	3	4	5	6	7	8	9	10	11	12
11	1	2	3	4	5	6	7	8	9	10	11	12	1	2	3	4	5	6	7	8	9	10	11	12
12	1	2	3	4	5	6	7	8	9	10	11	12	1	2	3	4	5	6	7	8	9	10	11	12
13	1	2	3	4	5	6	7	8	9	10	11	12	1	2	3	4	5	6	7	8	9	10	11	12
14	1	2	3	4	5	6	7	8	9	10	11	12	1	2	3	4	5	6	7	8	9	10	11	12
15	1	2	3	4	5	6	7	8	9	10	11	12	1	2	3	4	5	6	7	8	9	10	11	12
16	1	2	3	4	5	6	7	8	9	10	11	12	1	2	3	4	5	6	7	8	9	10	11	12
17	1	2	3	4	5	6	7	8	9	10	11	12	1	2	3	4	5	6	7	8	9	10	11	12
18	1	2	3	4	5	6	7	8	9	10	11	12	1	2	3	4	5	6	7	8	9	10	11	12
19	1	2	3	4	5	6	7	8	9	10	11	12	1	2	3	4	5	6	7	8	9	10	11	12
20	1	2	3	4	5	6	7	8	9	10	11	12	1	2	3	4	5	6	7	8	9	10	11	12
21	1	2	3	4	5	6	7	8	9	10	11	12	1	2	3	4	5	6	7	8	9	10	11	12
22	1	2	3	4	5	6	7	8	9	10	11	12	1	2	3	4	5	6	7	8	9	10	11	12
23	1	2	3	4	5	6	7	8	9	10	11	12	1	2	3	4	5	6	7	8	9	10	11	12
24	1	2	3	4	5	6	7	8	9	10	11	12	1	2	3	4	5	6	7	8	9	10	11	12
25	1	2	3	4	5	6	7	8	9	10	11	12	1	2	3	4	5	6	7	8	9	10	11	12
26	1	2	3	4	5	6	7	8	9	10	11	12	1	2	3	4	5	6	7	8	9	10	11	12
27	1	2	3	4	5	6	7	8	9	10	11	12	1	2	3	4	5	6	7	8	9	10	11	12
28	1	2	3	4	5	6	7	8	9	10	11	12	1	2	3	4	5	6	7	8	9	10	11	12
29	1	2	3	4	5	6	7	8	9	10	11	12	1	2	3	4	5	6	7	8	9	10	11	12
30	1	2	3	4	5	6	7	8	9	10	11	12	1	2	3	4	5	6	7	8	9	10	11	12
31	1	2	3	4	5	6	7	8	9	10	11	12	1	2	3	4	5	6	7	8	9	10	11	12

CLIENT INFORMATION

Name
Phone
Email
Website
Address
Billing Adress
City
State Zip
D.O.B
Business Hours

Additional Information

Name
Phone
Email
Website
Address
Billing Adress
City
State Zip
D.O.B
Business Hours

Additional Information

Name
Phone
Email
Website
Address
Billing Adress
City
State Zip
D.O.B
Business Hours

Additional Information

Name
Phone
Email
Website
Address
Billing Adress
City
State Zip
D.O.B
Business Hours

Additional Information

CLIENT INFORMATION

Name
Phone
Email
Website
Address
Billing Adress
City
State Zip
D.O.B
Business Hours

Additional Information

Name
Phone
Email
Website
Address
Billing Adress
City
State Zip
D.O.B
Business Hours

Additional Information

Name
Phone
Email
Website
Address
Billing Adress
City
State Zip
D.O.B
Business Hours

Additional Information

Name
Phone
Email
Website
Address
Billing Adress
City
State Zip
D.O.B
Business Hours

Additional Information

MEETING NOTES

SUBJECT	DATE	TIME

AGENDA

ATTENDEES

IMPORTANT NOTES

SUBJECT	DATE	TIME

AGENDA

ATTENDEES

IMPORTANT NOTES

MEETING NOTES

SUBJECT	DATE	TIME

AGENDA

ATTENDEES

IMPORTANT NOTES

SUBJECT	DATE	TIME

AGENDA

ATTENDEES

IMPORTANT NOTES

DECEMBER SELF-CARE

Write a self-care activity and tick off each time you do self-care act.

ACTIVITIES	CHECKLIST
	1 2 3 4 5 6 7 8 9 10 11 12 13 14 15 16 17 18 19 20 21 22 23 24 25 26 27 28 29 30 31
	1 2 3 4 5 6 7 8 9 10 11 12 13 14 15 16 17 18 19 20 21 22 23 24 25 26 27 28 29 30 31
	1 2 3 4 5 6 7 8 9 10 11 12 13 14 15 16 17 18 19 20 21 22 23 24 25 26 27 28 29 30 31
	1 2 3 4 5 6 7 8 9 10 11 12 13 14 15 16 17 18 19 20 21 22 23 24 25 26 27 28 29 30 31
	1 2 3 4 5 6 7 8 9 10 11 12 13 14 15 16 17 18 19 20 21 22 23 24 25 26 27 28 29 30 31
	1 2 3 4 5 6 7 8 9 10 11 12 13 14 15 16 17 18 19 20 21 22 23 24 25 26 27 28 29 30 31
	1 2 3 4 5 6 7 8 9 10 11 12 13 14 15 16 17 18 19 20 21 22 23 24 25 26 27 28 29 30 31
	1 2 3 4 5 6 7 8 9 10 11 12 13 14 15 16 17 18 19 20 21 22 23 24 25 26 27 28 29 30 31
	1 2 3 4 5 6 7 8 9 10 11 12 13 14 15 16 17 18 19 20 21 22 23 24 25 26 27 28 29 30 31
	1 2 3 4 5 6 7 8 9 10 11 12 13 14 15 16 17 18 19 20 21 22 23 24 25 26 27 28 29 30 31

REFLECTION

HOW WILL YOU RATE THIS MONTH? ☆ ☆ ☆ ☆ ☆ ☆ ☆ ☆ ☆ ☆

MONTHLY WINS	HOW DOES IT MAKE ME FEEL?
•	•
•	•
•	•
•	•

CHALLENGES	HOW CAN I IMPROVE IT?
•	•
•	•
•	•
•	•

ACCOMPLISHED GOALS	UNACCOMPLISHED GOALS	GOALS NEXT MONTH

HABITS RETAINED	HABITS ELIMINATED	NEW HABITS DEVELOPED

THREE THINGS THAT I AM MOST GRATEFUL FOR THIS MONTH

1	2	3

TWO LIFE LESSONS I LEARNED THIS MONTH

1	2

ONE WORD THAT BEST DESCRIBES THIS MONTH

WEEKLY PLANNER

WEEK OF

MOTIVATION

MON

TUE

WED

THUR

FRI

SAT

SUN

TO-DO

TOP PRIORITIES

NOTES

DAILY PLANNER

DATE S M T W T F S

TODAY'S GOALS

TODAY APPOINTMENT

Time	Event

SLEEP

MOOD

WATER INTAKE

Total :

EXERCISE

Total Minutes

Total Steps

THINGS TO GET DONE TODAY

MEAL TRACKER

Breakfast

Lunch

Dinner

Snack

REMINDER

TODAY I'M GRATEFUL FOR

NOTES

MONEY TRACKER

Money In	Money Out

DAILY PLANNER

DATE

S M T W T F S

TODAY'S GOALS

TODAY APPOINTMENT

Time	Event

SLEEP

MOOD

WATER INTAKE

Total :

EXERCISE

Total Minutes

Total Steps

THINGS TO GET DONE TODAY

MEAL TRACKER

Breakfast

Lunch

Dinner

Snack

REMINDER

TODAY I'M GRATEFUL FOR

NOTES

MONEY TRACKER

Money In	Money Out

DAILY PLANNER

DATE S M T W T F S

TODAY'S GOALS

TODAY APPOINTMENT

Time	Event

SLEEP

MOOD

WATER INTAKE

Total :

EXERCISE

Total Minutes

Total Steps

MEAL TRACKER

Breakfast

Lunch

Dinner

Snack

THINGS TO GET DONE TODAY

REMINDER

MONEY TRACKER

Money In	Money Out

TODAY I'M GRATEFUL FOR

NOTES

DAILY PLANNER

DATE

S M T W T F S

TODAY'S GOALS

TODAY APPOINTMENT

Time	Event

SLEEP

MOOD

WATER INTAKE

Total :

EXERCISE

Total Minutes

Total Steps

MEAL TRACKER

Breakfast

Lunch

Dinner

Snack

THINGS TO GET DONE TODAY

REMINDER

TODAY I'M GRATEFUL FOR

NOTES

MONEY TRACKER

Money In	Money Out

DAILY PLANNER

DATE S M T W T F S

TODAY'S GOALS

TODAY APPOINTMENT

Time	Event

SLEEP

MOOD

WATER INTAKE

Total :

EXERCISE

Total Minutes

Total Steps

THINGS TO GET DONE TODAY

MEAL TRACKER

Breakfast

Lunch

Dinner

Snack

REMINDER

MONEY TRACKER

Money In	Money Out

TODAY I'M GRATEFUL FOR

NOTES

DAILY PLANNER

DATE

S M T W T F S

TODAY'S GOALS

TODAY APPOINTMENT

Time	Event

SLEEP

MOOD

WATER INTAKE

Total :

THINGS TO GET DONE TODAY

EXERCISE

Total Minutes

Total Steps

MEAL TRACKER

Breakfast

Lunch

Dinner

Snack

REMINDER

TODAY I'M GRATEFUL FOR

NOTES

MONEY TRACKER

Money In	Money Out

DAILY PLANNER

DATE S M T W T F S

TODAY'S GOALS

TODAY APPOINTMENT

Time	Event

SLEEP

MOOD

WATER INTAKE

Total :

EXERCISE

Total Minutes

Total Steps

MEAL TRACKER

Breakfast

Lunch

Dinner

Snack

THINGS TO GET DONE TODAY

REMINDER

MONEY TRACKER

Money In	Money Out

TODAY I'M GRATEFUL FOR

NOTES

WEEKLY PLANNER

WEEK OF	
MOTIVATION	

MON	
TUE	
WED	
THUR	
FRI	
SAT	
SUN	

TO-DO

-
-
-
-
-
-

TOP PRIORITIES

-
-
-
-

NOTES

DAILY PLANNER

DATE S M T W T F S

TODAY'S GOALS

TODAY APPOINTMENT

Time	Event

SLEEP

MOOD

WATER INTAKE

Total :

EXERCISE

Total Minutes

Total Steps

THINGS TO GET DONE TODAY

MEAL TRACKER

Breakfast

Lunch

Dinner

Snack

REMINDER

TODAY I'M GRATEFUL FOR

NOTES

MONEY TRACKER

Money In	Money Out

DAILY PLANNER

DATE

S M T W T F S

TODAY'S GOALS

TODAY APPOINTMENT

Time	Event

SLEEP

MOOD

WATER INTAKE

Total :

EXERCISE

Total Minutes

Total Steps

THINGS TO GET DONE TODAY

MEAL TRACKER

Breakfast

Lunch

Dinner

Snack

REMINDER

TODAY I'M GRATEFUL FOR

NOTES

MONEY TRACKER

Money In	Money Out

DAILY PLANNER

DATE S M T W T F S

TODAY'S GOALS

TODAY APPOINTMENT

Time	Event

SLEEP

MOOD

WATER INTAKE

Total :

EXERCISE

Total Minutes

Total Steps

THINGS TO GET DONE TODAY

MEAL TRACKER

Breakfast

Lunch

Dinner

Snack

REMINDER

MONEY TRACKER

Money In	Money Out

TODAY I'M GRATEFUL FOR

NOTES

DAILY PLANNER

DATE

S M T W T F S

TODAY'S GOALS

TODAY APPOINTMENT

Time	Event

SLEEP

MOOD

WATER INTAKE

Total :

EXERCISE

Total Minutes

Total Steps

MEAL TRACKER

Breakfast

Lunch

Dinner

Snack

THINGS TO GET DONE TODAY

REMINDER

MONEY TRACKER

Money In	Money Out

TODAY I'M GRATEFUL FOR

NOTES

DAILY PLANNER

DATE S M T W T F S

TODAY'S GOALS

TODAY APPOINTMENT

Time	Event

SLEEP

MOOD

WATER INTAKE

Total :

EXERCISE

Total Minutes

Total Steps

MEAL TRACKER

Breakfast

Lunch

Dinner

Snack

THINGS TO GET DONE TODAY

REMINDER

MONEY TRACKER

Money In

Money Out

TODAY I'M GRATEFUL FOR

NOTES

DAILY PLANNER

DATE

S M T W T F S

TODAY'S GOALS

TODAY APPOINTMENT

Time	Event

SLEEP

MOOD

WATER INTAKE

Total :

EXERCISE

Total Minutes

Total Steps

MEAL TRACKER

Breakfast

Lunch

Dinner

Snack

THINGS TO GET DONE TODAY

REMINDER

MONEY TRACKER

Money In	Money Out

TODAY I'M GRATEFUL FOR

NOTES

DAILY PLANNER

DATE S M T W T F S

TODAY'S GOALS

TODAY APPOINTMENT

Time	Event

SLEEP

MOOD

WATER INTAKE

Total :

EXERCISE

Total Minutes

Total Steps

THINGS TO GET DONE TODAY

MEAL TRACKER

Breakfast

Lunch

Dinner

Snack

REMINDER

MONEY TRACKER

Money In	Money Out

TODAY I'M GRATEFUL FOR

NOTES

WEEKLY PLANNER

WEEK OF

MOTIVATION

MON

TUE

WED

THUR

FRI

SAT

SUN

TO-DO

TOP PRIORITIES

NOTES

DAILY PLANNER

DATE S M T W T F S

TODAY'S GOALS

TODAY APPOINTMENT

Time	Event

SLEEP

MOOD

WATER INTAKE

Total :

EXERCISE

Total Minutes

Total Steps

MEAL TRACKER

Breakfast

Lunch

Dinner

Snack

THINGS TO GET DONE TODAY

REMINDER

MONEY TRACKER

Money In	Money Out

TODAY I'M GRATEFUL FOR

NOTES

DAILY PLANNER

DATE

S M T W T F S

TODAY'S GOALS

TODAY APPOINTMENT

Time	Event

SLEEP

MOOD

WATER INTAKE

Total :

EXERCISE

Total Minutes

Total Steps

MEAL TRACKER

Breakfast

Lunch

Dinner

Snack

THINGS TO GET DONE TODAY

REMINDER

MONEY TRACKER

Money In	Money Out

TODAY I'M GRATEFUL FOR

NOTES

DAILY PLANNER

DATE S M T W T F S

TODAY'S GOALS

TODAY APPOINTMENT

Time	Event

SLEEP

MOOD

WATER INTAKE

Total :

EXERCISE

Total Minutes

Total Steps

MEAL TRACKER

Breakfast

Lunch

Dinner

Snack

THINGS TO GET DONE TODAY

REMINDER

TODAY I'M GRATEFUL FOR

NOTES

MONEY TRACKER

Money In	Money Out

DAILY PLANNER

DATE

S M T W T F S

TODAY'S GOALS

TODAY APPOINTMENT

Time	Event

SLEEP

MOOD

WATER INTAKE

Total :

EXERCISE

Total Minutes

Total Steps

MEAL TRACKER

Breakfast

Lunch

Dinner

Snack

THINGS TO GET DONE TODAY

REMINDER

TODAY I'M GRATEFUL FOR

NOTES

MONEY TRACKER

Money In	Money Out

DAILY PLANNER

DATE S M T W T F S

TODAY'S GOALS

TODAY APPOINTMENT

Time	Event

SLEEP

MOOD

WATER INTAKE

Total :

EXERCISE

Total Minutes

Total Steps

MEAL TRACKER

Breakfast

Lunch

Dinner

Snack

THINGS TO GET DONE TODAY

REMINDER

TODAY I'M GRATEFUL FOR

NOTES

MONEY TRACKER

Money In	Money Out

DAILY PLANNER

DATE

S M T W T F S

TODAY'S GOALS

TODAY APPOINTMENT

Time	Event

SLEEP

MOOD

WATER INTAKE

Total :

EXERCISE

Total Minutes

Total Steps

MEAL TRACKER

Breakfast

Lunch

Dinner

Snack

THINGS TO GET DONE TODAY

REMINDER

MONEY TRACKER

Money In	Money Out

TODAY I'M GRATEFUL FOR

NOTES

DAILY PLANNER

DATE S M T W T F S

TODAY'S GOALS

TODAY APPOINTMENT

Time	Event

SLEEP

MOOD

WATER INTAKE

Total :

EXERCISE

Total Minutes

Total Steps

MEAL TRACKER

Breakfast

Lunch

Dinner

Snack

THINGS TO GET DONE TODAY

REMINDER

TODAY I'M GRATEFUL FOR

NOTES

MONEY TRACKER

Money In	Money Out

WEEKLY PLANNER

WEEK OF

MOTIVATION

MON

TUE

WED

THUR

FRI

SAT

SUN

TO-DO

TOP PRIORITIES

NOTES

DAILY PLANNER

DATE S M T W T F S

TODAY'S GOALS

TODAY APPOINTMENT

Time	Event

SLEEP

MOOD

WATER INTAKE

Total :

EXERCISE

Total Minutes

Total Steps

THINGS TO GET DONE TODAY

MEAL TRACKER

Breakfast

Lunch

Dinner

Snack

REMINDER

TODAY I'M GRATEFUL FOR

NOTES

MONEY TRACKER

Money In	Money Out

DAILY PLANNER

DATE

S M T W T F S

TODAY'S GOALS

TODAY APPOINTMENT

Time	Event

SLEEP

MOOD

WATER INTAKE

Total :

EXERCISE

Total Minutes

Total Steps

MEAL TRACKER

Breakfast

Lunch

Dinner

Snack

THINGS TO GET DONE TODAY

REMINDER

MONEY TRACKER

Money In	Money Out

TODAY I'M GRATEFUL FOR

NOTES

DAILY PLANNER

DATE S M T W T F S

TODAY'S GOALS

TODAY APPOINTMENT

Time	Event

SLEEP

MOOD

WATER INTAKE

Total :

EXERCISE

Total Minutes

Total Steps

THINGS TO GET DONE TODAY

MEAL TRACKER

Breakfast

Lunch

Dinner

Snack

REMINDER

TODAY I'M GRATEFUL FOR

NOTES

MONEY TRACKER

Money In	Money Out

DAILY PLANNER

DATE

S M T W T F S

TODAY'S GOALS

TODAY APPOINTMENT

Time	Event

SLEEP

MOOD

WATER INTAKE

Total :

EXERCISE

Total Minutes

Total Steps

THINGS TO GET DONE TODAY

MEAL TRACKER

Breakfast

Lunch

Dinner

Snack

REMINDER

TODAY I'M GRATEFUL FOR

NOTES

MONEY TRACKER

Money In	Money Out

DAILY PLANNER

DATE S M T W T F S

TODAY'S GOALS

TODAY APPOINTMENT

Time	Event

SLEEP

MOOD

WATER INTAKE

Total :

EXERCISE

Total Minutes

Total Steps

MEAL TRACKER

Breakfast

Lunch

Dinner

Snack

THINGS TO GET DONE TODAY

REMINDER

MONEY TRACKER

Money In	Money Out

TODAY I'M GRATEFUL FOR

NOTES

DAILY PLANNER

DATE

S M T W T F S

TODAY'S GOALS

TODAY APPOINTMENT

Time	Event

SLEEP

MOOD

WATER INTAKE

Total :

EXERCISE

Total Minutes

Total Steps

MEAL TRACKER

Breakfast

Lunch

Dinner

Snack

THINGS TO GET DONE TODAY

REMINDER

TODAY I'M GRATEFUL FOR

NOTES

MONEY TRACKER

Money In	Money Out

DAILY PLANNER

DATE S M T W T F S

TODAY'S GOALS

TODAY APPOINTMENT

Time	Event

SLEEP

MOOD

WATER INTAKE

Total :

EXERCISE

Total Minutes

Total Steps

MEAL TRACKER

Breakfast

Lunch

Dinner

Snack

THINGS TO GET DONE TODAY

REMINDER

MONEY TRACKER

Money In

Money Out

TODAY I'M GRATEFUL FOR

NOTES

DAILY PLANNER

DATE

S M T W T F S

TODAY'S GOALS

TODAY APPOINTMENT

Time	Event

SLEEP

MOOD

WATER INTAKE

Total :

EXERCISE

Total Minutes

Total Steps

MEAL TRACKER

Breakfast

Lunch

Dinner

Snack

THINGS TO GET DONE TODAY

REMINDER

TODAY I'M GRATEFUL FOR

NOTES

MONEY TRACKER

Money In	Money Out

DAILY PLANNER

DATE S M T W T F S

TODAY'S GOALS

TODAY APPOINTMENT

Time	Event

SLEEP

MOOD

WATER INTAKE

Total :

EXERCISE

Total Minutes

Total Steps

MEAL TRACKER

Breakfast

Lunch

Dinner

Snack

THINGS TO GET DONE TODAY

REMINDER

TODAY I'M GRATEFUL FOR

NOTES

MONEY TRACKER

Money In	Money Out

DAILY PLANNER

DATE

S M T W T F S

TODAY'S GOALS

TODAY APPOINTMENT

Time	Event

SLEEP

MOOD

WATER INTAKE

Total :

EXERCISE

Total Minutes

Total Steps

THINGS TO GET DONE TODAY

MEAL TRACKER

Breakfast

Lunch

Dinner

Snack

REMINDER

MONEY TRACKER

Money In	Money Out

TODAY I'M GRATEFUL FOR

NOTES

NOTES

NOTES

NOTES

PLANNER
NIGHT PLANS
NIGHT PLANS